THE CHAMPIONSHIPS WIMBLEDON 1984

OFFICIAL ANNUAL

John Parsons

PAVILION
MICHAEL JOSEPH

First published in Great Britain in 1984 by
Pavilion Books Limited
196 Shaftesbury Avenue, London WC2H 8JL
in association with Michael Joseph Limited
44 Bedford Square, London WC1B 3DU

Copyright © 1984 The All England Lawn
Tennis and Croquet Club

Designed by Kieran Stevens

Parsons, John
   The Championships – Wimbledon:
   the official annual 1984.
   1. Lawn Tennis Championships
   I. Title
   796.342'09421'93   GV999

ISBN 0-907516-56-4

Printed and bound in Great Britain
by Butler & Tanner Ltd

FOREWORD

This is the second of what is intended to be a continuing series of Wimbledon Annuals. I am sure it will be welcomed by all those who want a permanent and comprehensive record of The Championships.

1984 will, I believe, long be remembered as a year when Dame Fortune smiled upon us in so many ways. With the exception of a chilling north wind early on and one or two very brief showers, the weather was ideal for the whole fortnight. Great crowds (over 30,000 up on the previous record), exciting matches of the highest standard and the presence of seventeen out of the twenty living Ladies' Singles Champions, all contributed to making it a very special year.

Indeed, the parade of the Lady Champions was an event that will live in the memory. After a nail-biting delay, the showery weather on the second Monday cleared. To a fanfare, followed appropriately and amusingly by 'Thank Heaven for Little Girls' played by the band of the Women's Royal Army Corps, the famous seventeen marched on and lined up. They were then introduced by Dan Maskell and each one came forward to be presented to The All England Club's President, His Royal Highness the Duke of Kent and his beautiful Duchess. Each champion got a huge cheer as she was presented with a specially engraved Waterford vase and the greatest cheer of all was given to our own Mrs Kitty Godfree, champion in 1924 and 1926, who, at the age of eighty-eight, is still playing tennis regularly.

For many people, 1984 conjures up Orwellian visions, but for those lucky enough to have been at The All England Club between 25th June and 8th July, it will mean a happy and memorable Championship year. This album will remind us in future years of the great time we had and for those who could not be there I believe the following pages will capture for them something of the magic of Wimbledon 1984.

R.E.H. Hadingham, O.B.E., M.C., T.D.
Chairman of The All England Club and the Committee of Management of the Lawn Tennis Championships

INTRODUCTION

Every year brings fresh energy and excitement to Wimbledon and the prelude to the 1984 staging of the world's greatest Championships was no exception. Quite apart from the magnificent tennis which was in prospect, there was the added delight of knowing that all but three of the twenty surviving lady champions, from the current holder Martina Navratilova to Kitty Godfree the winner sixty years ago, would be there to feature in The All England Club's celebrations of one hundred years of women's matches at Wimbledon.

It would be a chance to reflect and remember, as indeed would the further celebrations to mark the fiftieth anniversary of the first of Fred Perry's three consecutive titles in the men's singles.

As for the 1984 champion, only one name, Martina Navratilova, seemed to be in most people's minds. The bookmakers made her the most runaway favourite of all time and after the awesome manner in which she had just achieved the Grand Slam by winning the French Open, it was easy to understand their reasoning.

On the other hand it was also clear that Chris Lloyd, another great competitor as well as a magnificent champion, had been gearing her build-up in the first part of the year with Wimbledon principally in mind. After all, the only time she had defeated Miss Navratilova in their previous twelve matches had been on grass in Melbourne nineteen months earlier.

In the men's singles, although John McEnroe was clearly the favourite, Ivan Lendl and Jimmy Connors were not without their supporters. Would Lendl, we wondered, be able to follow-up his stunning victory over McEnroe in Paris from two sets down, by becoming the third Czechoslovakian in thirty years to conquer Wimbledon's grass?

Would McEnroe, without a Grand Prix tournament victory since Winbledon 1983, be able to justify his top seeding and keep his promise to 'let my racket do the talking', after all the disciplinary controversy in the week leading into The Championships? Or would Connors, the eternal fighter, prove his seemingly unquenchable resilience once again?

These and the regular search for new faces, coupled with the long-term forecast promising fine sunny weather for most of the Wimbledon fortnight, meant that the expectations on the first day of The Championships were as stimulating and exciting as ever.

As Bjorn Borg once said: 'The moment you walk through the gates on the first day there is a special atmosphere which hits you.' In part it is the occasion, in part it is the colour, but above all it is the knowledge that whatever happens over the next two weeks will genuinely become part of tennis history.

The fact that the defending champions were all back as top seeds in no way lessened the hopes – or indeed the speculation. It just tended to veer it slightly in other directions, such as guessing who, if anyone, might sustain the seven-year run of an unseeded player reaching the semi-finals of the men's singles. As we were to discover, that honour fell to Pat Cash in 1984.

For Wimbledon 1984, however, The Championships also had a new chairman, R.E.H. 'Buzzer' Hadingham who, during the days of rumbling controversy over players' behaviour just before the fortnight began, was to establish exactly the right mood of reasonableness among all concerned, as the day by day recollections of matches within these pages will show. His letter to John McEnroe at the start of the fortnight, welcoming him back to Wimbledon and assuring him that whatever he might have read, there would be no question of a disciplinary witch-hunt against anyone, did not go unappreciated.

Indeed at the end of The Championships, when the winners were being toasted at the Champions' Dinner, both Martina Navratilova and John McEnroe asked everyone to join them in a toast 'to Buzzer'. By doing so, they were also toasting the whole event.

It was that kind of rewarding Wimbledon when the cream rose to the top and even those whose feathers may have been ruffled at times along the way were left with a warming glow of satisfaction.

FIRST DAY

Monday 25 June

Opening day at Wimbledon can be rather like the start of a new year at school. A few of the old faces are missing. Some have been elevated from the masses to the rank of prefects inasmuch that they have been seeded for the first time. Others are discovering the special atmosphere and traditions of the place as a brand new, unnerving experience.

In the intimate world of tennis, the start of the oldest international championship is most of all a time for settling in, welcoming old friends and perhaps reflecting poignantly on a few fond memories from the past. In their different, equally fascinating ways, John McEnroe, Chris Lewis and Dick Stockton launched Wimbledon 1984 in precisely that manner.

Everywhere the hydrangeas looked at their best and the lush green of the lovingly manicured courts appeared even richer in the bright sunshine, as the first of nine record-day crowds familiarised themselves once more with the staircase they needed, how to get to Court 13 and, of course, the going rate for strawberries.

Naturally enough, at 2 p.m. precisely, the defending champion walked out on to the Centre Court. After all the hubbub of the previous fortnight, following problems for officials from McEnroe at Queen's Club, one hardly expected him to complete the knock-up without some disturbance.

In fact, in view of this, it was entirely predictable that McEnroe would set the tone for his entire progress through the tournament with barely a flicker of dissent. There were one or two moments when one clearly sensed he was biting his tongue or counting to ten but for the most part any McEnroe emotion was confined to a few withering looks or a shrug of the shoulders as he defeated Paul McNamee, the London-based Australian with the experience, as well as the game capable of causing an early upset, 6-4, 6-4, 6-7, 6-1.

There was one blue note by McEnroe. Apparently he had forgotten how Wimbledon still strictly applies the 'predominantly white' rule where clothing is concerned so there was quite some consternation when he walked out in front of the Duke and Duchess of Kent wearing blue shorts. McEnroe quickly disappeared to change.

McNamee, who had conscientiously put in twenty hours of practice with Australian left-hander Brad Drewett so as to be ready for the American, was asked later about McEnroe's chances of retaining his title. 'Of course he can be beaten here – but I don't think he will be,' he added prophetically. Asked who might upset the top seed, McNamee paused for several seconds and then replied, 'I honestly can't think of anyone.'

The 128 men in the Wimbledon draw consist of 104 who are high enough on the world ranking ATP-Atari computer to be accepted straight into the competition, 16 who fight their way through from the

Opposite: if there seems to be a look of concern, as well as concentration on the face of John McEnroe, one should not be surprised. Defending champions at Wimbledon have often found the early rounds their toughest battles and McEnroe found himself confronted by Australian Paul McNamee in his first round match, who has proved in the past that he can beat him. Looks, of course, can be deceiving.

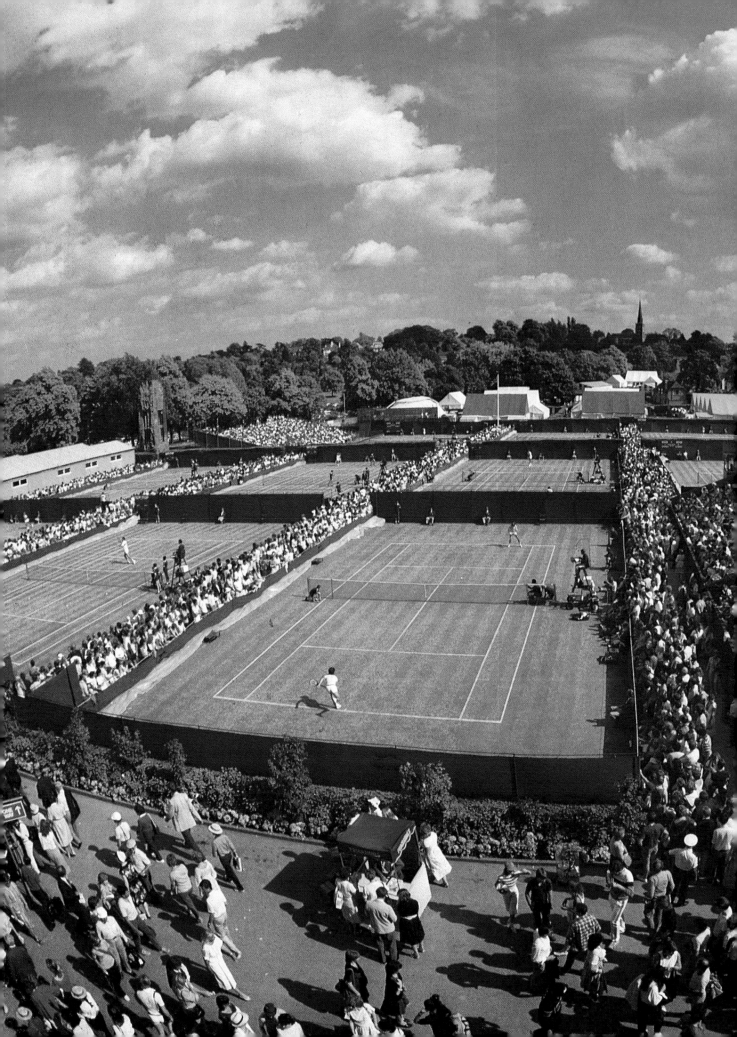

Preparing for and enjoying, with a touch of luxury, Wimbledon at its glorious best.

qualifying tournament for 128 others held at Roehampton, and eight 'wild cards' who are those, otherwise ineligible players, who the Committee of Management feels are worthy of special invitation. There can also be – as in 1984 – a few others who come in as 'lucky losers' from the qualifying tournament if a space is created by another player dropping out after the draw has been made but before his first match has started.

There will be much more to be said later about Carina Karlsson, the most impressive of this year's qualifiers. On Wimbledon's first Monday, however, Court 1 was occupied for approaching three hours by the only non-British man to receive a wild card – American Dick Stockton.

Stockton, the new coach to Trinity University in San Antonio, Texas and the current French Open mixed doubles champion with Anne Smith, was taken entirely by surprise at Wimbledon's way of thanking him for co-operating so willingly to play three mixed doubles matches in one day two years earlier, when rain threatened to make The Championships over-run.

Rediscovering glorious winners, as if plucked from the memory of his Wimbledon semi-final appearance twelve years ago, Stockton stretched second seeded Ivan Lendl almost to the limit. It was the closest match involving one of the tournament's principal performers since Bjorn Borg was taken to five sets by Victor Amaya in 1978. It was not until Stockton, who had been volleying delightfully, double faulted to go 2–4 down in the fifth set, that the Czechoslovakian, still elated by his victory in Paris at the French Open, could be sure of surviving this chilling first round lesson.

Lendl won 4-6, 6-0, 6-3, 5-7, 6-4. It was one of twenty first round matches in the men's singles to span five sets, but the first seed to depart, Anders Jarryd from Sweden, lost in four to Californian Scott Davis, whose concentrated power was to attract even wider attention later. As Yannick Noah had pulled out injured too late for him to be erased from the seedings and Jose-Luis Clerc withdrawn through 'illness', the casualty list among the seeds already totalled three.

Elsewhere on day one, Lewis, the previous year's unseeded runner-up to

McEnroe, one place too low to be seeded this time, retained quite a fan club for his first round defeat of Switzerland's Roland Stadler on Court 13. There were fanfares too for a flurry of British wins: Stuart Bale over John Alexander, Stephen Shaw against Claudio Panatta, and the more predictable ones for John Lloyd (albeit from two sets to one and a break down on Court 2, where he had never won before), Annabel Croft and Anne Hobbs. Wimbledon had started well.

Wimbledon's Peter Morgan reminds John McEnroe that his shorts hardly conform to the 'predominantly white' rule. A quick change followed. Ivan Lendl (opposite) needed and sought help from all quarters in his match against Dick Stockton.

Paul McNamee (left) and Dick Stockton (above) fighting to attract first day headlines. John Lloyd (right) launching the best Wimbledon run of his career.

Success all round.
Stuart Bale (left)
overcame the wily
John Alexander; Chris
Lewis (above) beat
Roland Stadler; while

(top) Scott Davis
provided the one
seeding upset of the
first day by beating
Sweden's Anders
Jarryd.

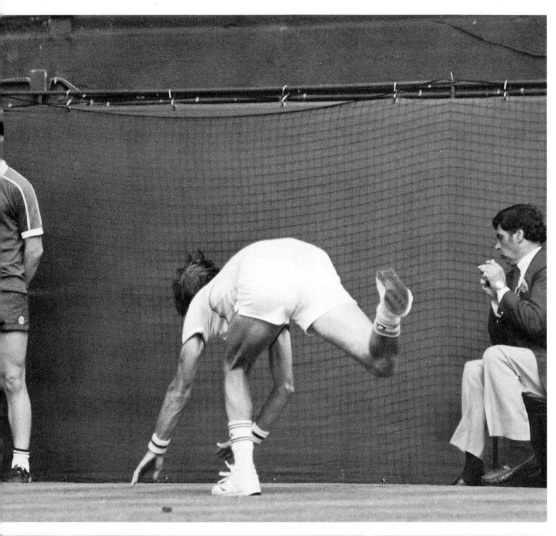

There's seldom a dull moment in any tournament when Jimmy Connors is on court. For more than a decade he had been throwing all his energy, determination and skill into every match he plays – but not even he can return everything an opponent offers. In this picture the racket may be reasonably close to the serve which Lloyd Bourne (left) has just fired, but the lunging Connors is still two or three strides away. An ace for Bourne.

Taking a leaf out of John Lloyd's book, the British women also started well. Anne Hobbs (far left) was too good for the American Federation Cup player, Candy Reynolds, while Annabel Croft (left) trounced the Swiss player, Petra Delhees-Jauch.

SECOND DAY

Tuesday 26 June

Ladies Day, to a large extent, developed into a British day. Martina Navratilova took one set to find her customary range and composure and then gave the Centre Court crowd a thrilling demonstration of her unmatched skill as she set off in defence of her title with a 6–4, 6–0 win over the likeable Californian, Peanut Louie. Chris Lloyd, one of only two other former champions in the draw, outclassed Sabrina Goles, while third seeded Hana Mandlikova, delicately expressing skill as well as power, out-played Elna Eliseenko from the USSR.

With the only three players who most people felt had any chance of being considered as the eventual champion safely through, the stage was cleared for Virginia Wade, the 1977 winner, to lead four other British girls into the second round, two of them after much excitement and trauma.

Miss Wade, playing in The Championships for the twenty-third time, starting before most of the 1984 seeded players were even born, was given a standing ovation when she recovered to beat the American, Ann Henricksson 3–6, 6–3, 6–4. Then on the same court, a packed, near hysterical crowd urged Sue Barker to a 2–6, 6–4, 6–4 defeat of South African Renée Mentz, following a disastrous start when she hardly kept a ball in play while losing the first five games.

Yet the real drama had still to come.

Jo Durie, the British number one, having ominously exposed all her fears and uncertainties by twice failing when she served for victory in the second set and then wasting a match point in the tie-break, discovered renewed mental strength to beat Kim Shaefer 6–2, 6–7, 6–0.

It was a rocky, roller-coaster ride by Miss Durie to revenge her defeat by the same American opponent a week earlier at Eastbourne, only a few hours after the Wimbledon draw had been made. Many a faint-hearted British fan abandoned the Centre Court after it all went so horribly wrong for Miss Durie in the second set. Oh ye of little faith!

The fourth British win of the day was certainly the least expected. Julie Salmon, 19, from Brighton, ranked 169 in the world, so needing a wild card entry, confidently served and volleyed her way to 6–4, 6–3, victory over Laura Arraya, a Peruvian ranked twentieth in the world and thought by many to be one of the most dangerous floaters in the draw. There was victory, too, for Amanda Brown over Vicky Nelson.

As for Miss Wade, dodging back and forth between matches, management committee duties, including the order of play and television commentating – she remained the favourite of the crowds and she seemed to speak for all the British winners when she remarked:

'It's great when they see British players win. I feel very privileged that they can

Opposite: for Jo Durie, it was a case of going through the mental and physical pain barrier more than once during her traumatic first round revenge clash with Kim Shaefer.

A tough opener for Peanut Louie (above) whose joy at playing on the Centre Court was probably tempered by the fact that it was against Martina Navratilova. No joy either for Peter Fleming (above right), overturned in the first round by Brad Gilbert.

still give me such applause. It's awfully nice out there in the sunshine and really, as I'm here, I might as well be in the tournament.'

As for her own match she said: 'I'm playing quite well but I haven't played many matches and I got very nervous when I was finally ahead.' Then while in full flow, answering another question at the Press conference, Miss Wade paused when a reporter sneezed. 'Bless you,' she remarked. How typical and how appropriate it seemed coming from an Archdeacon's daughter.

Meanwhile there was much passion and energy among the men as the first round was completed, bringing nine refugees from Roehampton and one lucky loser through to the second stage. Three matches were completed on Centre Court that day during 4 hours and 10 minutes of

brutal hitting on Court 1, as Bill Scanlon, a native of Dallas, survived a tremendous effort by Eric Korita, whose tennis was sharpened at Southern Methodist University in the same Texan city. Korita, a super-fit young man, lost despite serving 31 aces. The cheers at the end exceeded anything heard at Wimbledon throughout the fortnight, even in the finals.

It was just one of many long and demanding matches as three other seeds, Johan Kriek (against Michael Westphal), Tomas Smid (against Larry Stefanki) and Vitas Gerulaitis (against Tony Giammalva) were taken to five sets.

Perhaps the intensity of that last contest explains why the umpire forgot to enforce a change of ends at 4–1 in the second set, but no one seemed to mind. This year, happily, was one when most players concentrated solely on their tennis.

Above: happiness for
Sue Barker, however.
An amazing comeback
earned her victory
over South African
Renée Mentz, under
the watchful eye of
former champion
Billie-Jean King on
the players' balcony
(left).

Bill Scanlon (above) needed to apply all his resolute service return **skills to withstand a constantly fiery attack from Eric Korita (left).**

A classic study in concentration and effort from Tony Giammalva (left) who extended the 15th seed, Vitas Gerulaitis (right), over five eventful and immensely entertaining sets. Vitas, as usual, often took time out during changeovers to retape the grip of his racket – sharpening his teeth, perhaps, for the next game!

THIRD DAY

Wednesday 27 June

It is not often that British lawn tennis writers, however insular or partisan, find an excuse to concentrate their attention on British players two days in succession at Wimbledon, so it was a heartening, as well as a refreshing experience during the 1984 Championships to spend almost the whole of the first week wondering if the nation which gave lawn tennis to the rest of the world might at least be starting to raise its own standards again.

On Wednesday it was the turn of John Lloyd, Julie Salmon and Anne Hobbs to continue the brighter note already struck. Lloyd, in particular, was playing the most controlled, mature lawn tennis he had ever produced in the event, as he defeated the Californian, Greg Holmes, 4-6, 6-3, 6-4, 6-1.

Lloyd, 29, gave both a workmanlike and positive display, especially on his serve and volley as an overflowing Court 3, with spectators clinging precariously to any vantage point, however distant, watched him reach the third round for the first time since his Wimbledon singles debut in 1973. Then, he won £200. This win guaranteed him £3,850, almost twenty times as much. Tennis prize money, at least, manages to leap ahead of inflation.

As in their previous meeting at the US Open, Lloyd kept this former winner of the NCAA title in check. Despite Holmes's skilful double-handed hitting that produced spectacular passing shots through space where none apparently

existed, Lloyd outran and outranked his opponent with a sustained consistency which has not always been his forte.

Meanwhile the British girls, who by tradition have generally progressed much further than the men, were also winning patriotic cheers. Miss Salmon, the British junior grass court champion, beat the higher ranked Beverley Mould of South Africa 6-4, 7-6. In that second set tie-break, the increasingly confident Miss Salmon, employing a greater variety of shot, took it 7-0 before thrusting her arms aloft in triumph.

Miss Hobbs, full of aggressive agility, outlasted American Mary Lou Piatek, a former winner of the junior girls' singles at Wimbledon, ranked 39, principally because Miss Piatek's backhand briefly broke down under her opponent's pressure in the sixth game of the second set. Miss Hobbs won 6-4, 6-3.

Elsewhere among the ladies, there was only one major flurry of excitement. That was on Court 13 where Pam Shriver, a semi-finalist three years earlier and one of those big-hearted as well as big-hitting competitors you always feel will steal the show one day, was very nearly upstaged. At one point, Gigi Fernandez, 20, from Peru, a cousin of the film star José Ferrer, stood only two points from victory. The whole crowd round the court seemed to live and die that next point when the beleagured American escaped as Miss Fernandez nervously missed her target

Opposite: no, it's not John Lloyd! This handsome lookalike is in fact the American Leif Shiras; but despite his triumphs at Queen's Club, when he reached the final unseeded, Tim Gullikson stopped him in four sets in the second round.

29

with an easy smash. Miss Shriver, who benefited still further from the double fault which left her serving for the match, won 3–6, 6–3, 9–7.

The other half of Miss Shriver's world champion doubles partnership, Martina Navratilova, also looked less than comfortable for a spell while winning 6–2, 7–5 over the lively American, Amy Holton. Miss Holton was holding a point for 4–1 at one stage but a few moments later a ballboy handed the defending champion a note from one of her friends. A relaxed glow returned to Martina's appearance and to her tennis.

The crowds at Wimbledon, especially the younger generation, are always seeking new heroes and heroines. Leif Shiras, the John Lloyd look-alike from Milwaukee, was an obvious candidate this time, especially after his run at Queen's Club two weeks earlier when he went

through to become runner-up against John McEnroe. Tim Gullikson, however, the right-hander of the twins, made sure there was only limited opportunity on this occasion to enjoy the engaging personality as well as the tennis of the handsome American.

Gullikson progressed 3–6, 6–3, 6–4, 6–4 at more or less the same time as brother Tom was beating Britain's Stuart Bale, 7–5, 6–3, 6–4. One service break in each set decided this struggle between two left-handers. In essence, experience was the key.

Once again a few of the seeds wavered but survived. Jimmy Arias, for instance, over-seeded at five, considering that he had barely played on a grass court before this summer, needed five sets to beat Gianni Ocleppo, an Italian with the rare ability to thrive on fast courts. Yet he missed two great chances. Ocleppo lost

the first set after double faulting twice at 5–3. In the fourth set, when he was ahead two sets to one, he allowed Arias, who at times looked completely bewildered by the whole affair, to escape from 0–40 at 2–2.

Tomas Smid also needed five sets to stifle an exciting challenge from the Australian junior, Mark Kratzman, as did the twelfth seed, Johan Kriek, who recovered brilliantly to hustle the reigning world junior champion, Stefan Edberg, to a 4–6, 6–7, 6–4, 6–1, 6–1 defeat, mainly because the youngster's serve began to crumble.

No major problems though for Jimmy Connors or Ivan Lendl. Connors, seeded third, opened his shoulders powerfully to account for Stefan Simonsson and despite allegations that he may have opened his mouth a little too stridently as well, a re-run of the television film the next day completely exonerated him of any offence.

As for Lendl, his runaway victory over Derek Tarr from South Africa was briefly delayed when a family of young sparrows decided to have a game of their own just in front of the net on his side of the court as the Czechoslovakian was ready to serve. First he waved his racket at them; then he tossed some sawdust in their direction, but they were oblivious to such gentle persuasion. Eventually, when they were ready, they darted away. Lendl, who you might say had been tarred and feathered at the same time, waved them goodbye.

The day also guaranteed the presence of a qualifier in the last 16. Paul Annacone from New York dismissed Mark Dickson in one of the genuine upsets, while Christo Van Rensburg from Uitenhage, South Africa, defeated the Irish Californian, Matt Doyle, and so would face Annacone in the next round.

The first Wednesday of Wimbledon 1984 was almost a benefit day for British tennis. Julie Salmon (far left), Anne Hobbs and John Lloyd were only some of those who earned the patriotic cheers.

With nothing to lose, the young American Amy Holton was able to hit out and often keep Martina Navratilova at full stretch in this fascinating second round clash, when the champion might easily have dropped the second set.

Down – but not out. Pam Shriver (left) lost the first set and came perilously close to losing the third for the match, before escaping in the second round against Gigi Fernandez (above). Right: Tomas Smid had to pick himself up several times in fighting back from two sets to one down against the Australian junior, Mark Kratzman.

Stefan Edberg (left), the 1983 junior champion, who has already climbed into the world's top 25, explaining to the army of Swedish journalists (right) who follow their players on the circuit these days, how he missed out on claiming the scalp of 12th seeded Johan Kriek after taking the first two sets. Above: Gianni Ocleppo from Italy congratulates Jimmy Arias after the young American, so inexperienced on grass, had survived a five sets battle into the third round.

FOURTH DAY

Thursday 28 June

Despite the two short breaks for rain, the first at this year's Championships, the fourth day at Wimbledon was one of the finest – marvellous tennis almost everywhere one looked, outstanding triumphs for one or two of the old faces as well as the new, the first major upset among the seeds and, above all, what *The Guardian* called the 'Second wonder of Wade'.

Twelve days away from her thirty-ninth birthday, Miss Wade, the 1977 champion, earned a standing ovation, accompanied by a few tears in the Royal Box, as well as among the crowd and on the court, as she ousted Zina Garrison, the fifth seed, 3–6, 6–4, 7–5.

Rarely can Miss Wade have deserved the plaudits more. On the Centre Court where she has produced so many cheers as well as tears during her twenty-three playing visits to Wimbledon, she held on grimly early in the final set when Miss Garrison, the talented black player from Houston, had six chances to lead 4–1 and who at 5–4 was only two points away from the match.

No doubt the two stoppages, the first of fifty minutes, helped Miss Wade. 'Though I was doing the right things, I was not doing them properly,' said Miss Wade in recalling how she had lost the first set and was 2–1 down in the second when the first break became necessary. On the resumption she trailed 3–1 but then took four successive games, as she sensed that Miss Garrison had lost her momentum.

By the end of it all Miss Garrison's eyes were glazed with tears and Miss Wade, who, in some of her earliest Wimbledon years suffered the same disappointment and despair, said, 'I felt so bad for her.' In those days before she was champion, however, everything was in deadly earnest. Now, for the multi-talented Miss Wade, tennis is fun. In a way it is also easier.

Clearly, as in 1983, when she reached the quarter-finals, Miss Wade, who in her six previous tournaments during the year had recorded just one victory, was once more inspired by Wimbledon's enchantment. Annabel Croft, the Kent teenager, was just beginning to appreciate the magic of the place as well.

Miss Croft, still three weeks short of her eighteenth birthday and 1–4 down in the final set at the very moment the rousing cheers for Miss Wade's great triumph filtered across to her, responded by fighting back to beat the highly-rated American junior, Michelle Torres, 6–3, 2–6, 7–5.

Those spectators high up on the temporary stand around Court 13 could follow Miss Wade's progress on the Centre Court electronic scoreboard. At one point Miss Croft's umpire had to call for order when cheers broke out in the middle of a rally.

'I knew what was happening and it gave me a lift,' said Miss Croft, who for the previous ten days had been benefiting

Opposite: Annabel Croft, on her way to the exciting victory she recorded over Michelle Torres, with a little piece of inspiration transmitted from the crowd roaring Virginia Wade to victory on the Centre Court.

Elise Burgin (right) felt the strain as Jo Durie (above) began to get into her stride.

from Miss Wade's practical advice and assistance as a practice opponent. Suddenly those fierce forehands of Miss Croft began thumping a little more determinedly and the 'character and concentration' which Miss Wade had impressed upon her took over, especially when Miss Torres served for the match at 5–4.

With Jo Durie also reaching the third round with relative ease against Elise Burgin after her horrendous struggle two days earlier, it was another evening to toast British success, despite a gallant defeat for Stephen Shaw by Andres Gomez.

In the men's singles, John McEnroe advanced against Rodney Harmon, with no more than a fresh broadside in his battle to have courtside microphones removed. But the fears of fourth seeded Mats Wilander, that his interest in this year's Wimbledon might be brief, especially after his preparations had been sabotaged by a wrist injury, were sorrowfully confirmed for him by Pat Cash.

The injury could only partly account for Wilander's defeat. Cash, for instance, struck 15 aces and covered the court with tremendous pace, producing punishing volleys between a host of scintillating winners from the back of the court. His 6–7, 6–4, 6–2, 6–4 revenge of their

meeting in the Davis Cup final (also on grass in Melbourne the previous December) was an honourable one. It also pointed the way for other successes to come.

Another Australian, John Fitzgerald, who had been defeated by Wilander in a classic Wimbledon contest a year earlier, went out rather less spectacularly this time to Cassio Motta, while in another of those surprises which on a less eventful day would have attracted much more worthy attention, Frenchman Guy Forget, a qualifier, beat Canada's Glenn Michibata.

There was so much to see but so little time and many regretted being unable to linger for longer as the wonderfully elegant stroke-maker from India, Ramesh Krishnan, knocked out Chris Lewis, the athletic New Zealander who not only captivated Wimbledon but became an overnight superstar in his own country after reaching the final of the world's premier tennis event last year.

Krishnan graced the courts in a style established by his father, Ramanathan, two decades ago. Subtlety and placements, expressed with majestic precision, blunted the Lewis power and thrust, while the Krishnan lobs were a beautiful reminder of old-fashioned skills. It was like the soothing Port or Brandy at the end of an altogether adventurous, filling and spicey meal.

An exciting day in the men's singles. Stephen Shaw (above) stayed with Andres Gomez into tie-breaks in the first two sets, but there was a major upset as Pat Cash (right, above) exposed the limitations placed on Mats Wilander by his injury (far right, above). For Martina Navratilova and coach Mike Estep (left), the mixed doubles can also be a refreshing break.

Right: it may be raining, but these fans don't mind. The reason why is revealed overleaf.

Those spectators patiently huddling under the umbrellas were waiting for Virginia Wade to return to the Centre Court to continue play against Zina Garrison, the brilliantly talented though erratic player from Houston, seeded five, who was not even born when Miss Wade first started playing in these Championships. As Virginia was to admit later, the rain helped her. The first delay especially, when she was a set and 1–2 down, enabled her to rethink her strategy and then start turning the match around.

The exuberance of
Pat Cash, which was
to provide so many
exciting moments at
Wimbledon in 1984.

FIFTH DAY

Friday 29 June

History was made at Wimbledon on the fifth day – and not only because the attendance of 38,215 (only 76 below the all time record for any day) was the largest for any first Friday at The Championships. James Scott Connors, the champion in 1974 and 1982, who was in his thirteenth year of leaping, lunging and, in recent years, grunting his way through matches with totally uninhibited, free flowing vigour, registered his sixty-fifth victory in the men's singles.

His 6-4, 6-7, 6-3, 6-4 defeat of fellow American, Marty Davis, enabled him to beat the record held by Arthur W. Gore, Wimbledon's oldest champion, when he won the title for the third time in 1909. Gore's Wimbledon career spanned more than thirty-nine years.

It was just a pity that Connors, usually so ebullient and gregarious, only became his customary bright and breezy self in the fourth set. Others were less restrained, among them Paul Annacone, who became the guaranteed qualifier in the last 16 with his win over Christo Van Rensburg. 'I was just hoping I'd be the nobody who would do it', said Annacone, who had only turned professional on leaving Tennessee University a month earlier, and had just assured himself a first pay cheque from tennis of at least £6,850.

How did he feel about being at Wimbledon for the first time? 'This is every little tennis player's dream', he replied. 'This is where the dreams start.'

For someone who had set out in the first of three qualifying rounds at Wimbledon eleven days earlier, with a world ranking of 238, reaching the last 16 became far more than a dream.

Tim Mayotte could have appreciated how Annacone felt. He has always played well at Wimbledon and behaved well too, sustaining the nickname 'Gentleman Tim' he was credited with on his first visit. In reaching the fourth round as the only seeded player not to have dropped a set, with his 6-4, 6-3, 6-4 win over Tim Gullikson, Mayotte was given a new nickname by Connors, the man he would be facing next. He called him 'the sleeper' because he tends to reserve his best performance for Wimbledon each year. However, as we were to discover on the following Monday, Connors was more than alert to the threat which might have been posed.

The first two seeds beaten in the men's singles had both been Swedes. A third joined them, before their countrymen in the Press contingent or the crowd had started to take more than a passing interest in Miss Karlsson. Henrik Sundstrom, 20, though competing for the third time, was not able to tame Mark Edmondson, who had been dipping his feet in Wimbledon waters as far back as 1975, when Ken Rosewall and John Newcombe were still regularly around.

Eleven Americans, now that Johan Kriek has to be classified as such, reached the last 16, together with two from Czechoslovakia, one from Ecuador, a South African and an Australian. Hopes for a British representative at that stage vanished when John Lloyd, although playing to the best he was allowed, lost in straight sets to Scott Davis. As a junior, Davis, 21, broke the record for winning more American national titles than anyone else. The high promise he showed then has given him the foundation for the big, all court game, mixing fierce serving power with delightful touch, which gave the Wimbledon crowds a possible taste of stunning senior success which may soon be within his grasp.

Davis used his reach to such dramatic effect against Lloyd that the British

number two said it was like playing 'a telescopic man'. Certainly the Davis sights were set firm, as indeed were Ivan Lendl's as he celebrated his return to the Czechoslovakian Davis Cup team, confirmed a few hours earlier, by beating West Germany's Rolf Gehring 6–4, 6–2, 7–6.

John Lloyd's defeat in no way ruined the day for the British, however, any more than Julie Salmon's demise. She had moved into the deep waters ruled by more dangerous fish and, despite valiant resistance against an inevitable tide, lost 6–4, 6–3 to Kathy Jordan.

Such setbacks, both predictable, were after all overshadowed by the way Anne Hobbs had grabbed the opportunity to

Kathy Jordan

leap upon the British bandwaggon that was rolling with unusual success through the first week of Wimbledon, by knocking out the sixteenth seed, Carling Bassett of Canada.

A year earlier Miss Bassett had won the hearts of the Centre Court crowd with a charming victory over the Hungarian teenager, Andrea Temesvari. Since then neither have quite sustained their promise, Miss Temesvari largely because of the back problems she has endured and Miss Bassett because, like other teenagers suddenly launched into commercial, as well as sporting and human pressures, she has encountered difficult hurdles along the way.

Miss Hobbs, who defeated Miss Bassett 7–6, 6–4, won an opening set lasting 58 minutes on a drop shot on the fourteenth point of the tie-break, in a match which was a constant test of each player's nerves. There were 15 breaks of serve in 33 games but Miss Hobbs displayed the greater resolve when it mattered most, prompting an interesting observation from her opponent.

'How is it', asked Miss Bassett, 'that the British play so well here and are mediocre everywhere else? It's as if God's putting a spell on them.' As Jo Durie was a 1983 semi-finalist in Paris and Flushing Meadow, Miss Bassett's comparison lacked some credibility but after five successive days of unexpected British joy, one could understand how she felt.

Julie Salmon

The lively and personable Betsy Nagelsen (left), who has recorded some of her most famous victories over the years on grass, enjoyed herself by taking the second set from the former champion, Chris Lloyd.

Paul Annacone (left), still on the outside courts but on the way to upholding the recent tradition of qualifiers in upsetting the rankings. Above, right: Althea Gibson, the 1957–58 ladies' champion, seated just below Chris Lloyd, seems to share John Lloyd's acknowledgement that Scott Davis, the 'telescopic man', was just too good for him on the day.

SIXTH DAY

Saturday 30 June

Not for the first time in recent years (one remembers Ilie Nastase then the top seed, losing there to Sandy Mayer in 1973 and John McEnroe to Tim Gullikson in 1979), Court Two was a centre of action and incident on the middle Saturday of Wimbledon 1984.

In the opening match there, Bill Scanlon was leading 6-2, 2-6, 7-6, but a break at down 1-2 in the fourth set, when Boris Becker, 16, a strapping young qualifier from West Germany, had to retire with torn ankle ligaments. He was flown home that night and operated upon two days later.

Moving in to play a volley, Becker, the youngest competitor in the men's singles, who by ironic coincidence had benefited from an injury retirement by Nduka Odizor in the previous round, stumbled and fell. Despite immediate attention, it was obvious that he would be unable to continue, thereby destroying his hopes of joining Steffi Graf, 15, also from West Germany and the youngest competitor in her event, through to their respective fourth rounds. Miss Graf had achieved this distinction with a whole string of fine passing shots while beating Bettina Bunge. Miss Bunge was born in Switzerland, later qualified for West Germany while living in Florida, but at Wimbledon was listed as being from Monaco. There are times these days when players seem to switch countries as frequently as they switch their brand of racket.

After the premature end to the Scanlon-Becker match, Court 2 was then occupied for nearly three hours by Virginia Wade and the little known Carina Karlsson, under the rapt attention of not only a packed crowd within the Court but on every inch of space on the players' balcony, their tea room windows and vantage points which no one knew even existed before.

In a long, enthralling battle, in which Miss Wade led 5-3 in the final set and twice served for the match, the pertly attractive Miss Karlsson kept fighting back and eventually pinned down her opponent with superb groundstrokes, deep into the corners on both flanks. Miss Wade gave everything she had. Miss Karlsson, oblivious it seemed to the occasion and the British crowd, urged herself constantly to greater effort and in the 17th game, on the fourth break point, she achieved the service break which proved decisive, winning 6-2, 4-6, 11-9. It was tennis theatre of the highest quality. Equally it was genuine sport at its unrivalled best. After her astonishing win over Zina Garrison in the previous contest, Miss Wade had said, 'I just hope I don't have a letdown in the next round.' It certainly was not that. She had run and battled with just as much enthusiasm as an opponent eighteen years her junior, until the stamina, not the heart, gave out.

Quality in fact was the order of the day. Jo Durie produced her best tennis of

Opposite: Carina Karlsson – for once the Swedish men were overshadowed.

the week, especially her retrieving on the backhand, in advancing to the fourth round for only the second time in her career with a 6–4, 6–2 win over the American Kim Steinmetz. And Annabel Croft, who was then to concentrate her mind on a long but triumphal week in the junior competition, illustrated how her game, as well as her approach, had matured, by extending Chris Lloyd to a 6–3, 6–4 victory for the second seed, often by-passing her renowned opponent from the baseline.

In the men's singles, John McEnroe and the other four seeds left in the top half of the draw all came through, although Gomez had a fierce battle with Guy Forget and Kevin Curren needed every ounce of his well-proven power, especially on the serve, to stifle the wily ploys of Ramesh Krishnan. It was yet another impressive display by the Indian, whose tennis, like that of his fellow countryman, Vijay Amritraj, can be such a joy to watch but somehow just lacks a little of that extra steel necessary to bring the rewards it often deserves.

There was an element of tragedy about Curren's victory. The previous evening he had heard from his home in South Africa that his father, who appeared to have made a full recovery from a heart attack earlier in the year, had died suddenly. In consultation with the family, Curren decided to play on at Wimbledon in both singles and doubles and the funeral was postponed until he returned just over a week later. Knowing how proud Mr Curren was of his son's success in tennis, there is no doubt that Kevin carried out what would have been his wishes.

So, at the end of the first week, eleven of the seeds remained in the men's singles, the largest number since 1970, leaving the line-up for the main battles still to come as follows: McEnroe v Scanlon; Gerulaitis v Sadri; Cash v Curren; Moor v Gomez; Annacone v Kriek; Mayotte v Connors; Arias v Smid and (Scott) Davis v Lendl.

In the women's singles only four of the 16 seeds had departed and the second week programme read: Navratilova v Sayers; Hobbs v Maleeva; Shriver v Potter; Turnbull v Jordan; Graf v Durie; Sukova v Mandlikova; Karlsson v Temesvari and Kohde-Kilsch v Lloyd.

Clearly there would be more than enough drama there to keep the news

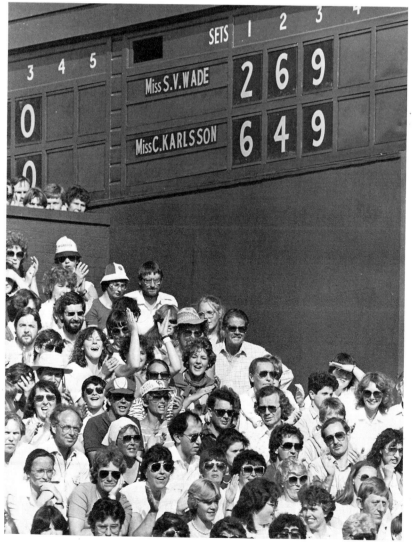

It was one of the most gripping contests of the fortnight, which could have gone either way. In the end Miss Karlsson achieved the finest win of her career. For Miss Wade, the disappointment at the end of her 23rd Wimbledon was evident.

journalists as well as the tennis orientated Press occupied, although just in case, and conscious of the strong feelings being expressed by some of the players, both publicly and through the Women's Tennis Association and Association of Tennis Professionals, The All England Club took the unprecedented step over the weekend of issuing a statement condemning certain Press harassment of players. Fortunately there was a much happier event at the start of the second week to steer moods and emotions back on to an even keel.

A match for the connoisseur, but the silky skills of Ramesh Krishnan (far left) were checked by Kevin Curren (left), one of the semi-finalists in 1983. Right: disaster for 16-year-old West German Boris Becker, whose magnificent challenge to Bill Scanlon came to an abrupt end in the fourth set when he seriously injured his ankle.

Not since the legendary Suzanne Lenglen won in 1925 has France produced the winner of the women's singles. There are exciting new French prospects coming along however, not least the bubbly, hard-hitting Catherine Tanvier (left), who was unlucky to find Hana Mandlikova in one of her more consistent moods when they met in the third round. The 6–4, 7–6, scoreline illustrates how close it was. Right: Jo Durie's coach Alan Jones, a significant influence on her game, watches her comfortable victory over Kim Steinmetz.

SEVENTH DAY

Monday 2 July

Below right: Martina Navratilova, first of seventeen winners who were each presented with a specially engraved Waterford vase by the Duke and Duchess of Kent. Below: Jo Durie recreates, at the Hurlingham Club, how it was one hundred years before. Right: Kitty Godfree, the oldest surviving champion, who stole the show.

In one sense it was a bitter disappointment when the second Monday of The Championships dawned with an overcast sky, which gradually became darker until, ninety minutes before the ladies' singles champions of the past were due to parade on the Centre Court, it rained.

In one sense also, however, the delay, albeit a brief one of forty-five minutes, was appropriate. After all, in 1884 when, against the wishes of many, thirteen ladies took part in the first women's singles, they had to wait several days until the men had finished their competition before they were allowed to start.

No such sexual discrimination remains today. Indeed, with the sun breaking through just as the Duke and Duchess of Kent walked out onto the Centre Court for the start of the Centenary presentations, Wimbledon became wonderfully and unashamedly awash with nostalgia and emotion.

As the band of the Women's Royal Army Corps followed up a fanfare with 'Thank Heaven for Little Girls', defending champion Martina Navratilova, arm in arm with All England Club committee man, Basil Hutchins, led out the line which unfolded like a rich tennis tapestry.

Martina and former champion, Chris Lloyd, who were both staying in private homes close to the Club, virtually within hailing distance of each other, had been comparing notes over breakfast as to what they should wear. Their choice of blouses

64

The Centenary Celebrations. Left to right: Virginia Wade, the most recent British champion, Billie-Jean King, holder of the record number of titles, and a general salute to memories past before the Duke and Duchess of Kent return to the Royal Box.

Below: a line-up of tennis history. Left to right, back row: Virginia Wade, Evonne Cawley, Angela Mortimer, Maria Bueno, Margaret Court, Ann Jones, Chris Lloyd, Martina Navratilova. Front row: Althea Gibson, Doris Hart, Margaret du Pont, Alice Marble, the Duchess and Duke of Kent, Kitty Godfree, Pauline Betz, Louise Brough and Shirley Fry.

and slacks raised a few eyebrows in some quarters until Althea Gibson, champion from 1957-8, appeared in sporty blue blazer and white slacks, beaming broadly and waving excitedly to the crowds.

For all the champions there was a handshake from the President and a beautifully engraved commemorative piece of Waterford glass. For many, particularly those champions she has watched most often, there was also a kiss on both cheeks from the Duchess.

It was like a family reunion, to which the Centre Court crowd and millions more watching on television were privy. And more than a few tears were shed. After Martina and Chris, there was Billie-Jean King, Virginia Wade, Evonne Goolagong, smiling as sunnily as ever, Margaret Court and Ann Jones.

Only three of the surviving twenty champions were missing - the two Helens, Wills and Jacobs, and Karen Susman - as generations spanning sixty years came to

honour an event which began a hundred years earlier. Then Maud Watson, daughter of a country parson, defeated her elder sister, Lilian, in the first final.

There was Maria Bueno, full of the beauty and elegance which marked her tennis, Angela Mortimer, the first British champion since the war, Miss Gibson, and then more memories of the dominant American era from Shirley Fry, Doris Hart, Louise Brough, Margaret DuPont and Pauline Betz. The late Maureen Connolly was also surely there too, in spirit.

As the ladies took their bows and made their curtseys, one by one, the only two pre-war champions were left until last of all. First came the vivacious Alice Marble, stepping out smartly and finishing up with a kiss for Dan Maskell, the Master of Ceremonies.

Finally, there was Kitty Godfree. It was exactly sixty years since Mrs Godfree, then Miss McKane, won Wimbledon for the first time and there was more than just

admiration and affection for this upright old lady in the rousing reception she was given.

In some ways Mrs Godfree, aged 88, who still plays tennis twice a week and who, the day after the parade was to nip away with Jean Borotra, 86, for a few gentle games of mixed doubles, epitomised at that poignant moment the traditions, the stability and the standards which are the hallmark of Wimbledon.

Somewhere in the early minutes of The All England Club, there is a comment which reads 'It is not desirable to have a ladies cup played for under any circumstances.' The events of 1884 altered all that, proving that even in those days, Wimbledon, for all its staid reputation, led the way whenever there was need for change. One cannot help wondering, nevertheless, whether the fact that the Ladies' trophy is that magnificent silver gilded plate, instead of a cup like the rest, was something of a nineteenth century compromise.

While the great ladies, past and present, were on parade, the second week of The Championships was already under way, offering possibly the richest feast of tennis in one day which even Wimbledon has ever offered. Four of the top five seeds remaining in the men's singles and three of the top four in the women's singles, all faced matches which one would have expected to test their nerve as well as their skill.

In the event, only one of them faltered. Jimmy Arias, despite improving round by round in his apprenticeship year on grass, lost in straight sets to Tomas Smid, the thirteenth seed. Smid is also happier on clay, but so successful and experienced on carpet that perhaps this was not the greatest surprise.

The genuine upsets, both among the men and the women came elsewhere as Paul Annacone and Carina Karlsson made sure that for the first time, there would be both a male and female qualifier in the quarter-finals. Several men have achieved such progress in the past, among them John McEnroe, who went on to the semi-finals in 1977 as a qualifier, but Miss Karlsson became the first woman to do so with her splendid 6–4, 7–5 victory over fifteenth seeded Andrea Temesvari. It was yet another astonishing performance by the Swedish girl as she raised her game still further against the taller and more

Three unseeded players made it to the last eight of the men's singles, among them Paul Annacone (opposite, top) who overwhelmed Johan Kriek (opposite, below) with almost astonishing ease, and John Sadri (left). Although seen here playing a winning volley, Sadri mainly had his outstanding service power to thank for his defeat of Vitas Gerulaitis.

For the second
successive year, John
McEnroe ruthlessly
dispelled the idea that
he could be upset at
Wimbledon by the
Texan Bill Scanlon,
who has been known
to upset him in more
ways than one in other
surroundings. It must
have been something
of a lonely, as well as
thoughtful walk back
through the tunnel for
Scanlon from Court 1
after his chastening
straight sets defeat.

Right: Tim Mayotte,
who has consistently
impressed at
Wimbledon, also had
hopes of creating an
upset, but after a
bold, aggressive first
set, he was just as
firmly outplayed by
the ebullient Jimmy
Connors, seen
overleaf.

powerfully built Hungarian, who was stunned to find herself being aced seven times. The more she played the easier it became to spot the impact Bjorn Borg has had on Swedish tennis. Miss Karlsson even wore the trademark headband while applying her aggressive, mightily impressive groundstrokes from the baseline.

Annacone, meanwhile, although arriving late from the number two dressing room, where he had been ensconced, quickly made up for lost time, setting such a blistering pace that twelfth seeded Kriek, 26, was never allowed an opportunity to find any rhythm for his game. The former sociology student from East Hampton, New York, crowded the net at every opportunity and kept Kriek on the run with a barrage of volleys and smashes. In fact Kriek was under such pressure that in pushing for extra authority on his serve he was broken five times and slipped to a 6–3, 6–2, 6–4 defeat.

There were two other seeding upsets. John Sadri, a former runner-up in the Australian Open, won eighteen consecutive points on his own most formidable serve in the first set which gave him an early initiative as he steadily wore down Vitas Gerulaitis over five strenuous sets. Then Pat Cash, oozing confidence and with enormous energy in his tennis, shrugged off the loss of the first set to beat the 1983 semi-finalist, Kevin Curren, 4–6, 6–2, 7–6, 6–1 in a contest full of fast, instinctive and gripping exchanges.

Elsewhere, you might say, the status quo was maintained. John McEnroe easily defeated his arch rival, Bill Scanlon, without any of the cross words which had been bandied about in the forty-eight hours since they knew they would be playing each other. Perhaps the appointment of a woman, Mrs Georgina Clark, to umpire the match, was a timely reminder to both of them that Wimbledon expected everyone to behave.

McEnroe did more than that. He produced a near perfect display of serving and, helped by the number of times Scanlon dropped his deliveries short, won endless service return winners as well. Andres Gomez smartly dealt with unseeded Terry Moor, who had been enjoying his finest run at any major event and Jimmy Connors, who, after losing his

opening serve said he was 'seeing the ball as big as a basketball', crushed Tim Mayotte with surprising ease, 6–7, 6–2, 6–0, 6–2.

The only favourite forced to struggle was Ivan Lendl. He went a break down at the start of the tense final set and it was only when he served for the match a second time that he disposed of Scott Davis, who, as against John Lloyd and Anders Jarryd, had served and volleyed with a magical combination of touch and skill. Then at 4–4 in the final set both men went through agonies of nerves. First Lendl broke serve brilliantly, then Davis promptly did exactly the same. At 5–5, 0–30, the still defiant Davis flew, almost horizontally, to play an incredible stop volley winner. But it was the last point he was to be allowed.

Among the women, the most excitement was undoubtedly on Centre Court, where Jo Durie, again walking a tightrope in near despair at times, squeezed her way into the quarter-finals for the first time with a 3–6, 6–3, 9–7 victory literally bludgeoned out of fifteen-year-old Steffi Graf. It was only on her third match point, when she was also serving for the match that Miss Durie finally broke her young opponent's astute and controlled resistance.

There were times when Miss Durie looked magnificent, others when she could have been a novice. Miss Graf fed on such inconsistency. She was so secure from the back of the court, so accurate with her groundstrokes, while her coolness on big points was astonishing. The two backhand crosscourt winners she produced to deny Miss Durie her first two match points were full of class and character.

Anne Hobbs, Britain's other hope, made a determined-enough effort, as the 6–2, 3–6, 6–3 scoreline suggests, but was too often deterred from trying to establish the net control she needed by the success of Manuela Maleeva's forehand passes.

Martina Navratilova had a long wait after the parade to get on court and was only kept there a few minutes for after losing the first set, her Australian opponent, Elizabeth Sayers, 0–6 down, retired with a gastric illness. Two other American serve and volley specialists also advanced, Pam Shriver against her keen, equally aggressive rival, Barbara Potter, and Kathy Jordan over Wendy Turnbull, while Hana Mandlikova was too good for Helena Sukova. Chris Lloyd's match against Claudia Kohde-Kilsch, delayed first by the parade but also by the weather, did not get on court at all.

Martina Navratilova shows her concern as Australian Elizabeth Sayers is forced to quit after struggling to overcome illness during the first set of their match.

EIGHTH DAY

Tuesday 3 July

On the eve of her twenty-second birthday, Pam Shriver had hoped to beat Kathy Jordan and thereby earn another crack at her doubles partner, Martina Navratilova in the semi-finals. In retrospect Miss Shriver should have won, for she had ample chances to break her opponent's serve. Miss Jordan, however, coached by Judy Dalton, had both the talent and tenacity to fight her way through in the one quarter-final of the women's singles which went against the odds.

The others, one has to admit, were not only straightforward but also lacking in emotional appeal, even if the calibre of the tennis from the winners merely confirmed their right to be listed as the finest players in the world. Manuela Maleeva, 17, who had beaten Chris Lloyd in the final of the Italian Championships, is justifiably regarded as one of the soundest players from the back of the court, but not even she could seriously begin to cope once Miss Navratilova took charge, almost at will, at the net.

Delightful though she looked in her pretty dress, trimmed in lemon and with ribbon in her hair, Miss Maleeva's occasional double-handed backhand crosscourt winners were but minor irritations to the champion in so chillingly effective a mood. Miss Navratilova won 6-3, 6-2.

For several months, ever since she beat the world number one in Oakland, Hana Mandlikova had been expressing increased belief in her own ability to upset Miss Navratilova anywhere at any time. In the opportunities presented to her since the Californian upset she had not quite managed to do so but the way she set about defeating Jo Durie 6-1, 6-4, won even more converts to the message she had been preaching.

Throughout the first set and to 2-0 in the second, Miss Mandlikova played as if she was the expert providing a carefree exhibition. Winners simply flowed with sweetness and joy from her racket. Then, as so often happens, her mind seemed to wander and Miss Durie, who had looked to be heading for a defeat of embarrassing proportions, jumped in to take four games in succession. At 30-30, while serving for 5-2, however, Miss Durie, who had suddenly moved into the most impressive groove she had managed at any time during the fortnight, slipped and fell, losing the point in the process. She was not hurt but her confidence was jarred and although she also had a point for 5-3 in the eighth game, the British revival was over.

So Miss Mandlikova, her heart set on beating Miss Navratilova, went into the semi-finals, where she might first have to play Chris Lloyd. One cannot help wondering if the psychological warfare was already biting deeply into the second seed, making her simmer with indignation over apparently being overlooked.

Certainly there was a much sharper

Not all the stars at Wimbledon are on the courts. Showbiz personalities Bruce Forsyth (left) and Terry Wogan relax between matches on women's quarter-final day when Martina Navratilova once more demonstrated her attacking power, this time over Manuela Maleeva (right).

edge to Mrs Lloyd's play as she accounted for Claudia Kohde-Kilsch in their postponed fourth round clash, 6–2, 6–4, than there had been in any of her earlier matches. Miss Kohde-Kilsch, who had pressed Miss Navratilova so closely at Eastbourne two weeks earlier, was constantly in two minds about whether to challenge from the back of the court or at the net. In the end Mrs Lloyd gave her no choice by dictating almost every exchange.

Meanwhile most of the other events were by now well under way and one of the fondest memories of this day was to be on Court 3 as two dapper figures, Ken Rosewall, 49 and Frew McMillan, 42, walked out to a standing ovation for a match in the '35 and Over' singles. Rosewall won, but his legs were no longer able to carry him fast enough into the shots he wanted to play against Marty Riessen a day later. Nevertheless, one brief glimpse of Rosewall is always better than none at all.

Pam Shriver can always be sure of one celebration at Wimbledon. Her birthday, on July 4th, always falls at some stage during the fortnight, but this time the anniversary was clouded by her quarter-final defeat by Kathy Jordan on this day. Kathy, who knocked out Chris Lloyd in 1983, certainly had something to celebrate this year as well.

Jo Durie (right), despite a strong second set, was forced to bow to the most impressive match Hana Mandlikova (below) played during The Championships, while Claudia Kohde-Kilsch (left) with high hopes after her fine performances at Eastbourne, could not match either the skill or the experience of Chris Lloyd.

NINTH DAY

Wednesday 4 July

Three players arrived at Wimbledon on the ninth day with the opportunity to maintain a record that stretched back over each of the previous seven years – that of reaching the semi-finals unseeded. In the event only Pat Cash did so, moving one stage closer to the jackpot by defeating Andres Gomez 6-4, 6-4, 6-7, 7-6. By doing so, Cash, the former world junior champion who had won the junior title at Wimbledon two years earlier, became the youngest Australian ever to reach the last four at these Championships. When Ken Rosewall first did so in 1954 he was nineteen-and-a-half, six months older than this latest well-muscled, self-reliant young man who had made such a buoyant impact throughout the competition.

Cash won with a vigorous display of sustained serving and positive play at the net and it was a pity that an otherwise superb contest also brought the only penalty point which had to be issued in the whole fortnight. Gomez, unhappy with two decisions in the first game of the fourth set, expressed himself in a manner which the umpire, who had already warned him for ball abuse, could not overlook.

When Gomez who, for a man raised on clay had played with such fine attacking zeal over the fortnight, took the fourth set to a tie-break, he must have felt he was still in with a fine chance of winning. After all he had also won the third set on a tie-break, 7-3, to maintain his record in winning all of his thirteen tie-breaks before that, stretching back to March.

This time, however, with Cash hitting every stroke with absolute authority and zest, the Gomez tie-break touch ran out and the Australian, with the thighs of a weightlifter supplying the power for his energy, went on to snare his third seed.

One of the toughest matches John McEnroe ever played in his life was against John Sadri in the final of the NCAA Championships in 1978. McEnroe won in four sets but only after being aced thirty times. Since then, these two Americans have generally been in different tennis worlds, McEnroe constantly at the top, Sadri switching in and out of lower levels. The distinction was only too obvious as McEnroe, having hit four successive winners off Sadri's normally penetrating serve in the second game of the match, swept through 6-3, 6-3, 6-1.

It was the end of an adventurous first Wimbledon journey too for Paul Annacone. In the opening game against Jimmy Connors he struck one shot so fiercely that it took the racket clean out of his opponent's grasp but after losing three chances to break the former champion in the fifth game, Centre Court nerves seemed to get through to the young pretender and the rest of his challenge was basically a token one. Connors won 6-2, 6-4, 6-2.

Ivan Lendl also progressed in straight sets, 6-1, 7-6, 6-3 against fellow

Opposite: the established order, both in world rankings and Czechoslovakian tennis was maintained as second seeded Ivan Lendl knocked out his fellow countryman, Tomas Smid (overleaf).

Czechoslovakian Tomas Smid but only after berating experienced line judge Georgina Clark, accusing her of being 'deaf and blind' for, in his mind, not seeing a serve from Smid which was clearly in the tramlines. Still seething later over what he felt was a harshly imposed warning, Lendl gave vent to a catalogue of complaints which when examined in detail could not in fact be substantiated. There will always be inconsistent treatment in life, none more so than when one person collects a parking ticket and the next in line does not. Yet few places try harder than Wimbledon to make sure any apparent favouritism is not intentional.

While it was the men who occupied centre stage most of the time on the ninth day, there was also one piece of unfinished business in the quarter-finals of the women's singles and in this Chris Lloyd provided the Centre Court gallery, including Princess Diana, H.R.H. The Princess of Wales, with a scintillating display by defeating Carina Karlsson, 6–2, 6–2.

The headline in *The Times* the next

Smid was beaten in just over an hour and a half, while in about the same time John Sadri (near right) was outclassed by John McEnroe. Despite the look of self-disgust that McEnroe is trying to mask, it was one of the very few unforced errors he made as he easily rebuffed the threat of the Sadri serve.

morning read 'The governess gives the waif a lesson she will never forget'. Certainly Mrs Lloyd, competing in her thirteenth Wimbledon (as was Jimmy Connors, who followed her on court), played the matriarchal role perfectly. The intimidating combination of the former world champion in severe form *and* playing on the Centre Court for the first time was all too much for the delightful Miss Karlsson, whose natural exuberance steadily ebbed away in the second set.

It had been, like most of Wimbledon 1984, another fascinating, rather than epic day, but it was still not over. Indeed the irrepressible Cash had another contribution to make. He and Paul McNamee, who the day before had been taken to five exhilarating sets by Ken Flach and Robert Seguso, were locked at two sets all against Mark Edmondson and Sherwood Stewart, when, at 8.40 p.m. and with the Duke and Duchess of Gloucester still watching avidly, play was suspended.

The crowd wanted the match to continue. So Cash, still in high spirits after his singles triumph, leapt over the net and received a singles serve from his partner, which he promptly lashed high up into the stands. The crowd roared with delight, gave the players a standing ovation and went home happy.

The sporting Andres Gomez still manages to raise a smile as he congratulates Pat Cash as the Australian becomes the youngest player from that country ever to reach a Wimbledon semi-final.

The Princess of Wales, with All England Club Chairman, R.E.H. 'Buzzer' Hadingham in the Royal Box on the Centre Court, on the first of her two visits to Wimbledon this year.

July 4, 1984

Lt. Col. Peter B. Webster
All England Lawn Tennis Club
Wimbledon

Dear Col. Webster:

Wimbledon is the most prestigious and coveted tournament in the world. Players consider it a privilege to compete here and we all look forward to the championships with added enthusiasm and excitement.

Many factors contribute to a successful event. One of them is the officiating, which is absolutely essential to ensure fair play and a fine tournament.

On behalf of the Women's Tennis Association, I would like to extend a sincere congratulations to you and your associates for such an outstanding effort this year. Thanks to your diligent work, the players have been allowed to perform at their highest levels, and Wimbledon has been witness to the best tennis possible.

For this, the WTA and more than 150 players who have competed during this fortnight thank you with our deepest appreciation.

Kind regards

Chris Evert Lloyd

Chris Evert Lloyd
President, WTA

July 4, 1984

Mrs. C. Evert Lloyd,
President,
Women's Tennis Association,
c/o The All England Lawn Tennis Club,
Wimbledon.

Dear Mrs. Evert Lloyd,

Thank you so much for your kind letter to-day.   To the best of my knowledge this is the first time such a message has been sent by those playing at Wimbledon to those who have the pleasure of officiating for them.

We are delighted that our efforts to achieve a high standard of work here have received such positive recognition from those whose skills we respect and admire so greatly.   I can assure you that our Umpires will be most encouraged by your letter.

Thanks to the excellent co-operation and sportsmanship displayed by your members, Wimbledon 1984 has been a happy and successful event.   We are very pleased if we have made some little contribution towards this.

Our best wishes to you all for the remainder of this tournament and for the future.

With kind regards,

Peter Webster

Lt.Col. P. B. WEBSTER,
Chief of Umpires,
Wimbledon Championships.

Chris Lloyd's involvement with Wimbledon can spread beyond her matches. On the day when she caught up with the other women and won her way through to the semi-finals with a thoroughly convincing defeat of Carina Karlsson, she also wrote, in her capacity as President of the Women's Tennis Association, to the group of Wimbledon officials so often taken for granted, thanking them for their efforts.

TENTH DAY

Thursday 5 July

Hana Mandlikova will not easily forget semi-finals day for the women at Wimbledon in 1984. Reaching heights of accuracy, consistency and all round excellence which many had started to feel she would never be able to scale again, Chris Lloyd summarily dismissed an opponent who can vary from being awesome to awful, 6–1, 6–2.

The match – and you could hardly call it that – was over in forty-five minutes. And with Martina Navratilova only marginally less emphatic in her 6–3, 6–4 defeat of Kathy Jordan in sixty-seven minutes the huge gulf in women's tennis between the top two and the rest was plain for all to see.

Neither challenger did herself justice. Miss Mandlikova, who constantly set herself up as a bewildered target at the net for Mrs Lloyd to pass with relish, collected only eight points, two of them double faults, on the American's serve. Miss Jordan, not playing badly but not playing well enough either to break Miss Navratilova's attacking style, managed only seven.

There was no doubt that Mrs Lloyd felt she had a point to make after all the comments from Miss Mandlikova about how she felt she could beat Miss Navratilova in the final. 'I think that maybe Hana underestimated me', she said. 'When people do that and write me off, I just come through', Mrs Lloyd added, perhaps remembering the 1981

final, when she also beat Miss Mandlikova with clinical ruthlessness, against most of the forecasts.

Miss Mandlikova went into the match knowing she had to be aggressive and accurate. In the event she was neither and some of her sorties to the net amounted to suicide runs. In fact although she moved to the net on fifty-two occasions, she won no more than seventeen points in the process.

It was small wonder at the end that Miss Mandlikova wanted to depart from the scene as quickly as possible, but in sweeping off without waiting for Mrs Lloyd she only further damaged her reputation and her standing with the Women's Tennis Association. After she had declined to attend interviews, which in the WTA's eye are mandatory, they applied a £350 fine.

The one consolation had been to see Mrs Lloyd's game flourishing so beautifully again. She took charge from the moment she broke in the third game, starting to hit stunning winners to all points and corners of the court and the first set was all over in twenty minutes. Even when she created openings, Miss Mandlikova seemed powerless to put them away. Mrs Lloyd knew only too well how to deal with the opportunities she had. Whereas Miss Mandlikova was constantly kept guessing by Mrs Lloyd, particularly on whether the passes were going crosscourt or down the line, the

Opposite: Kathy Jordan on the run – as most players are when they face Martina Navratilova. Hard though she fought, Miss Jordan, who deserved her seven games, was only able to glean seven points off the champion's serve.

A winning overhead
from Martina
Navratilova, who had
first opened up the
whole court.

A day to forget for
Hana Mandlikova but
a victory to cherish
for Chris Lloyd, as
the American
spectacularly lifted her
game back to the
highest plane.

Another example of the total dominance which Martina Navratilova can impose on a match – Kathy Jordan can do little more than wait apprehensively at the net as her opponent decides where she is going to hit the ball.

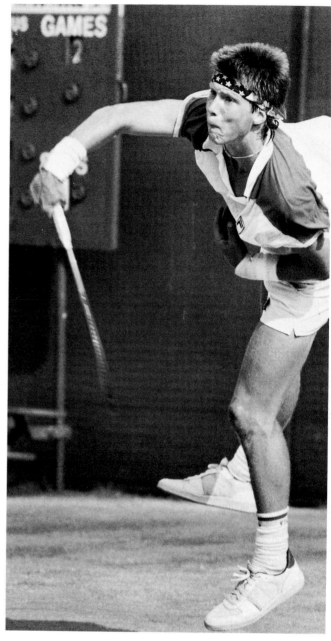

Above: Luke Jensen, the American junior, with a unique style all of his own.
Opposite, top: the Fred Perry statue, unveiled this year.
Below: Jean Borotra presents Fred with a silver salver to mark the 50th anniversary of his first Wimbledon crown. The Perry family – Fred, his wife Bobby and daughter Penny – admire the magnificent cake which was later given to the ballboys and girls for their party.

former champion, moving with renewed zip and zest, was royally in command.

Elsewhere meanwhile, the day provided more than usual interest in the junior boys' singles. The sight of young American, Luke Jensen, serving right-handed from the deuce court and left-handed from the advantage court, not to mention playing rallies ambidextrously as well, created much attention. So too did Eric Winogradsky from France. His 7–6, 6–2 defeat of Patrick McEnroe which meant that like Jensen, he reached the quarter-finals, will enable him, in years to come, to claim a remarkable distinction.

He will be able to say that on successive days he beat Nastase and McEnroe at Wimbledon – and it will be true. The day before knocking out John McEnroe's

young brother, Eric defeated Ilie Nastase's nephew, Mihnea. However both he and Jensen fell at the next hurdle.

Of course it was not only the centenary of women's tennis which was being celebrated at Wimbledon. It was also the fiftieth anniversary of the first of three successive wins in the men's singles by Fred Perry, the last British champion. The 'Perry Gates', now adorning Somerset Road and the statue of Fred greeting everyone on the lawns as they enter The All England Club, had been unveiled a few weeks earlier by the Duke of Kent.

The formal celebration, however, was marked at a splendid dinner-dance party in the Members Enclosure at The All England Club after close of play on the second Thursday, given by Fred and his wife Bobby for more than three hundred and fifty friends they had made during a lifetime in sport. All aspects of tennis were represented and Jean Borotra, on behalf of 'The Four Musketeers' – himself, Rene Lacoste, Henri Cochet and the late Jacques Brugnon – presented Fred with an inscribed salver to mark this great occasion.

Other sports and walks of life were also represented. Henry Cotton, who fifty years earlier had won the British Open golf title, boxer Henry Cooper, cricketers Denis Compton, Fred Trueman, Godfrey Evans and Tom Graveney, Peter Ustinov and Derek Nimmo, were among those who heard club chairman, R.E.H. 'Buzzer' Hadingham toast Fred and announce the arrival of a huge birthday cake which next day was sent to the ballboys and girls for their party.

Nothing seemed to have been overlooked, right down to the last detail. Even the glazed chicken breasts were decorated with the Perry laurel wreath. Sidney Wood, the champion of 1931, who had flown from America that day and was returning next morning by Concorde to host his daughter's wedding party, spoke for everyone when he said, 'I wouldn't have missed it for anything.'

ELEVENTH DAY

Friday 6 July

A fox, they say, is seldom more dangerous than when he is wounded. If ever there has been a wily old fox in tennis in recent years it has surely been Jimmy Connors, with the inspirational winners and finger-wagging rebukes he so often manages to produce if he thinks an opponent has stepped out of line.

Certainly Connors must have felt somewhat wounded going into his semi-final against Ivan Lendl. Stretching back over their previous three encounters (one, in Rotterdam, interrupted and never completed because of a bomb scare) Connors had lost the last twenty consecutive games. He was in no mood to let that sequence continue in the Wimbledon semi-final.

Discovering, as he had so often done before, reserves of energy and spirit for the great occasion, and despite losing the opening set on a tie-break, Connors responded with typical aggression, courage and bravado to win 6-7, 6-3, 7-5, 6-1.

The aggression was obvious in almost every shot Connors played, especially the way he threw himself into returning – often as winners or at least as the foundation of a point he won – services by Lendl which, against almost any other player, would themselves have been decisive. It shone through in the fierce, flat, full-length groundstrokes which he used to keep Lendl under pressure and prevent the Czechoslovakian establishing

any real dominance at the net.

The courage was best revealed in the way Connors turned the match round after a first set, played in blistering heat, during which the American must have devoured so much internal energy on every point that many of us wondered if he could last the pace.

It was here that the bravado came in. There was no doubt during the third set, in which Lendl led 3-1, that both men were beginning to tire, which was hardly surprising. Yet while Lendl, looking increasingly drawn and gaunt, could not hide his feelings – indeed there were moments when he appeared on the point of collapse – Connors masked his suffering magnificently and roared on with the adrenalin flowing even more strongly.

There were two major moments in that third set. The first was when Connors, despite Lendl's fifteenth ace, broke back in the fifth game. The other was at 5-5, 15-15 when, at the end of a brief exchange of shots at the net, Lendl played what he had every reason to assume would be a winner but Connors, darting forward with a defiant lunge, responded with the most glorious backhand angled return which just curled back over the net.

The little war dance and the shaking of the fists which Connors produced then – his only show of extravagant delight during the afternoon – illustrated that Connors knew then that the match would be his. Indeed it was. For much of the

Opposite: although beaten in three sets, Pat Cash pushed John McEnroe as hard as anyone during the fortnight.

There were many exciting and athletic points in this semi-final, although McEnroe always seemed to have something in reserve.

fourth set Lendl played more from instinct than belief. In the first three sets there had been seventeen aces and only two double faults from the second seed. In the fourth set there was just one more token ace and four double faults as Connors plundered gleefully on.

It was, for the most part, a highly enjoyable as well as excitingly competitive match, except for one incident, late in the second set when the American's insistence on always having the last word as well as the last point, might have led to him turning a trivial incident into a serious one.

Upset by a service call, which led to him being warned for holding his nose to show what he thought about the decision, Connors claiming he had only been scratching it. He went to umpire Malcolm Huntingdon and tried to bluff his way out of it by saying 'Why don't you relax, man? If you want to play the power game and get me out of this event, just say the word and I'll quit now. I don't think you would like that to happen with 15,000 people here.'

Huntingdon, showing more sense than the player, chose to ignore the remark *and* the demonstration Connors then gave to illustrate the difference between scratching his nose and making a rude gesture.

Nevertheless, Connors richly warranted the chance to go through to the final where, as almost everyone had predicted, John McEnroe would also be in attendance. Doggedly though Pat Cash fought in the second semi-final, the Australian was never seriously in with a chance of diverting the other left-handed American from a victorious path and McEnroe won 6–3, 7–6, 6–4.

The second set might have gone the other way. McEnroe, with so much time to play his shots and design the rallies, became surprisingly lackadaisical for a while, but whenever he needed to lift his game, as when Cash had broken for a 2–0 lead in the second set, he did so. It was the same in the tie-break. Cash led 4–1 but lost it 7–5.

Not that we knew it then but, despite that set he dropped to Paul McNamee in the first round, this was the match which tested McEnroe's reactions more than any other during the fortnight. On finals day two years earlier, while McEnroe and Connors were slogging it out for a record 4 hours 16 minutes, Cash was just beginning to make his mark by winning the junior title. One expects to enjoy and admire much from him again.

Cash has the ability to be a champion of the future. At Wimbledon 1984 however, McEnroe, the complete player, was always the master.

For many, this was
the most memorable
match of the fortnight.
Both Jimmy Connors
and Ivan Lendl were
full of explosive
confidence during a
tremendous first set.

'Just relax,' says
Connors, who has
always had the ability
to break the tension in
a match. Lendl isn't
exactly convinced that
it's only a game.

The heat was on and
the pressure was
starting to tell.

There was no let up in the pace but Connors, blazing away on almost every point, began to take control.

THE FINALS

Saturday 7 July and Sunday 8 July

At the Champions' Dinner to mark the end of Wimbledon in 1983, Sir Brian Burnett, then Chairman of The All England Club, had described Martina Navratilova and John McEnroe as two outstanding champions. In retaining their titles in 1984, they were not only to reinforce that recognition but to enhance their reputations as being among the best for all time.

Wimbledon somehow makes it a habit of inspiring something special for the greatest occasion. A British win for Virginia Wade at the Championships' centenary in 1977 was a classic example. It was absolutely right, therefore, that in the year of the women's centenary, the title should go to the player currently greatest in the game. Equally it was fitting that to win, Miss Navratilova should have been engaged in a sparkling, often enthralling contest with Chris Lloyd, who had also been the best in her time.

It was a far closer and much more memorable struggle than most had dared to expect, especially as Miss Navratilova, with eleven successive wins over her great rival, had most recently been defeating her with almost cavalier ease. But this time the champion had to rise to her peak, in terms of resilience and power, to win 7-6, 6-2.

Mrs Lloyd, Wimbledon champion three times, began quite brilliantly in her bold, imaginative bid to prevent Miss Navratilova becoming the first player since Billie-Jean King (1966-68) to win the title for three successive times. She hit a variety of telling shots which, for the first time in the fortnight made Miss Navratilova feel unsure - and her forehand suspect. In next to no time Mrs Lloyd led 3-0, with two breaks.

By the fifth game, however, the Navratilova power was beginning to re-assert itself, especially the sting and depth which it brought to the serve. Most of all it came to the rescue with an ace when Mrs Lloyd had a break point at 4-4, which could have left her serving for the set. Then, in the tie-break, after Mrs Lloyd had double faulted at 2-5, another ace settled it for the champion on her third set point.

Although limited to eight games, the second set was only marginally less taxing and interesting than the first, with both players producing superb tennis, despite the hundred degree heat in the bowl of the Centre Court. For once the weather, the tennis, the venue and the occasion perfectly matched and complemented each other.

It was an historic final, too, controlled for the first time by a woman umpire, Georgina Clark, from Oxfordshire, and an all-woman team.

The result meant that Miss Navratilova and Mrs Lloyd were then level at 30-30 in victories against each other. 'Believe it or not, I wish we would quit right now and never play each other again', said the winner. 'It's just not right for one of us to say that she's better than the other.'

The £90,000 and the title belonged to Miss Navratilova but much of the honour also went to Mrs Lloyd, who had raised her game to the peak she always knew was still there, even though some waited for the evidence to be convinced. It was a great final.

In a way the men's singles final was great too - but only for the devastating manner of McEnroe's 6-1, 6-1, 6-2 defeat of Jimmy Connors, at a time when both were seeking their third title. From the moment McEnroe alternately stroked and thumped four successive winning serve returns past Connors in the second game, Connors seemed to sense he could be in for one of the great humiliations of his tennis life in a major event.

Even allowing for the fact that, at 31, there had not been time for him fully to replenish the energy he had needed to beat Lendl forty-eight hours earlier, Connors seemed to be accepting the inevitable long before the end. Far from seeing the ball as big as a basketball as he had earlier in the tournament, there were times against McEnroe when he hardly saw it at all. It was not like him to make no effort at all to reach some shots, no matter how hopeless the bid might have been.

On the other hand he simply could not cope with the style and dexterity of the McEnroe serve, which was to decide, either immediately or from the first volley, sixty per cent of the points. In becoming the first American since Donald Budge in 1938 to retain the title, McEnroe also gained the easiest victory, certainly in terms of games, since that match forty-eight years earlier, when Budge trounced Bunny Austin 6-1, 6-0, 6-3 on his way to the first Grand Slam.

Budge, who had been present throughout the fortnight, described McEnroe's tennis as being that of 'a

Opposite: Chris Lloyd, whose marvellous challenge to Martina Navratilova made it the most exciting women's singles final for years.

For once even the newly crowned Grand Slam champion found herself under acute pressure as Mrs Lloyd eagerly attacked from the net.

genius at work'. So it was, even though most also shared Budge's disappointment that Connors was unable to vary the tactics which were proving so horribly wrong.

For McEnroe it was the completion of a remarkable triumph as much over himself, and his difficulty at times (but not this year) in controlling his emotions, as over any of the opposition he shrugged aside along the way. The only time in the final when his concentration even remotely strayed was at the end of the second set. Briefly, he recalled the disaster which befell him after he had been similarly placed in the final of the French Open against Lendl four weeks earlier.

'I purposely tried to stay calm and save all my energy for the match', he said later. 'In Paris I wasted a lot of energy getting angry with myself and that hurt me. That is something I learned. When I play like I did today. I can beat anyone.'

No one would argue with that. He had kept his promise of the opening day, 'I'll let my racket do the talking.'

So with the main finals completed, it was time to tidy up the rest and, for the first time in the history of The Championships, the top seeds and the

defending champions were all triumphant. There were, therefore, two titles each again for Martina and John.

McEnroe had already made sure of his first the day before retaining the singles crown, when he and Peter Fleming were extended, largely through their own making, to five sets by Pat Cash and Paul McNamee, before winning 6–2, 5–7, 6–2, 3–6, 6–3. McEnroe was the dominant player and personality in the match. McNamee's serve was broken three times, Cash's and Fleming's twice – but the Australians only once even reached deuce against McEnroe's serve.

It was the fourth Wimbledon win for the Americans, one less than that achieved by John Newcombe and Tony Roche in the late 1960's and 1970's. Meanwhile another, barely known Australian pair, Peter Doohan and Michael Fancutt, came through as the first lucky losers to reach the semi-finals, beating the experienced Gullikson twins, Tim and Tom along the way, before losing a five sets thriller to Cash and McNamee.

Martina Navratilova returned to the Centre Court immediately after the men's doubles final to retain the women's doubles title with Pam Shriver. They

dropped only one set in six matches – against Hana Mandlikova and Claudia Kohde-Kilsch in the quarter-finals – and the final in which they defeated Kathy Jordan and Anne Smith, the winners in 1980, lasted a mere fifty-four minutes.

There was the prospect at one time of Miss Navratilova becoming the first player since Billie-Jean King in 1973 to win three titles. Her mixed doubles partnership with her coach, Mike Estep, was a formidable one but Sherwood Stewart and Elizabeth Sayers knocked them out in the quarter-finals.

Instead, to the obvious delight of a still packed Centre Court crowd, one of the major titles went, at least in part, to Britain, when John Lloyd and Australian Wendy Turnbull (recently awarded the M.B.E.) kept the mixed doubles trophy. Despite having to play two matches on successive days when the programme slipped behind, in deference to players involved in other events, they first overcame Stewart and Miss Sayers, in their toughest struggle and then Steve Denton and Kathy Jordan, 6–3, 6–3 in the final.

There was some compensation for Stewart when he and Marty Reissen won

the '35 and Over' doubles, defeating Colin Dibley and Jaime Fillol in the final. For Dibley, though, this meant a second runner-up prize for he also lost to Stan Smith in the final of the '35 and Over' singles.

Finally to the juniors, where two South Africans, Stefan Kruger and Elna Reinach, 15, reached the final round but victory went to Mark Kratzman, the blond, left-handed Australian, rated so highly by John Newcombe, and to Annabel Croft, 17, the first British winner of the junior girls' title since Ann Jones won in 1956.

Kratzman, as already mentioned, had pushed thirteenth seeded Tomas Smid to five sets in the second round of the main event after winning his way into the tournament from the qualifying round. Miss Croft had made it to the third round in the senior singles and showed her fighting qualities by winning both the semi-finals and final in the junior event after being a set down.

For the British, at least, there could not have been a happier finish to a Wimbledon which drew record crowds of 391,673 and demonstrated once again its pre-eminent position in the game of lawn tennis.

**Total commitment
gives way to sheer
delight when the battle
is over and Martina
becomes champion for
the fifth time.**

Jimmy Connors would never admit it, but he must have been a trifle apprehensive as he faced this repeat of the 1982 final, which he won. John McEnroe had won the last 13 sets they had played in their many meetings – and it was not long before Connors must have realised that there was unlikely to be any relief from that sequence.

Right from the start
the McEnroe serve
was to dictate the
match.

For all his efforts, Connors could not summon up the energy he needed. He was seldom in the right place at the right time and McEnroe punished him time and time again for his over-zealous belief that he could win from the net.

The cup, once again, for McEnroe; commiserations from the President of The All England Club for Connors.

Many happy returns for Wendy Turnbull and John Lloyd, popular and entertaining winners once again in the mixed doubles competition.

Urgent consultations between Paul McNamee and Pat Cash, but they too were unable to find the answer to John McEnroe's dominating serve as he and Peter Fleming once more proved themselves the finest men's doubles pair in the world.

Kathy Jordan and Anne Smith (volleying) renewed their partnership this year after Miss Smith's brief spell in retirement, but in a one-sided final they had no answer to the awesome combination of Martina Navratilova and Pam Shriver who a month earlier, in Paris, had completed a doubles Grand Slam.

Farewell to Commander Charles Lane, who, at the age of 81, retired after 18 years of making sure that the ballboys and girls at Wimbledon are the envy of the world. He was honoured on the Centre Court where the Duchess of Kent presented him with a commemorative clock.

Twelve years after winning the men's singles title, in that memorable final against Ilie Nastase, Stan Smith (right) won the 35 and over invitation singles final from the 1983 champion in this event, Colin Dibley. Dibley was on the losing side again when he and Jaime Fillol lost the final of the 35 and over doubles, despite this tumble by Sherwood Stewart right in front of his partner, Marty Riessen (above).

Annabel Croft, the first British winner of the junior girls' singles since Ann Jones, smiles proudly from the Royal Box with her trophy. Below: the boys' champion, Mark Kratzman from Australia, receives his trophy from the Duke of Kent, while (right) Peter Fleming and John McEnroe congratulate each other on retaining the men's doubles title once again.

Left: Martina Navratilova and Pam Shriver with the trophy they have held continuously since the summer of 1981.

Above: Wendy Turnbull and John Lloyd completed the unique champions' record at Wimbledon 1984.

Overleaf: John and Martina celebrate in style at the Champions' Dinner, held at the Savoy.

CHAMPIONSHIP RECORDS 1984

THE CHAMPIONSHIP ROLL

Champions and Runners-Up

MEN'S SINGLES

1877—S. W. Gore
W. C. Marshall
1878—P. F. Hadow
S. W. Gore
★1879—J. T. Hartley
V. St. L. Goold
1880—J. T. Hartley
H. F. Lawford
1881—W. Renshaw
J. T. Hartley
1882—W. Renshaw
E. Renshaw
1883—W. Renshaw
E. Renshaw
1884—W. Renshaw
H. F. Lawford
1885—W. Renshaw
H. F. Lawford
1886—W. Renshaw
H. F. Lawford
★1887—H. F. Lawford
E. Renshaw
1888—E. Renshaw
H. F. Lawford
1889—W. Renshaw
E. Renshaw
1890—W. J. Hamilton
W. Renshaw
★1891—W. Baddeley
J. Pim
1892—W. Baddeley
J. Pim
1893—J. Pim
W. Baddeley

1894—J. Pim
W. Baddeley
★1895—W. Baddeley
W. V. Eaves
1896—H. S. Mahony
W. Baddeley
1897—R. F. Doherty
H. S. Mahony
1898—R. F. Doherty
H. L. Doherty
1899—R. F. Doherty
A. W. Gore
1900—R. F. Doherty
S. H. Smith
1901—A. W. Gore
R. F. Doherty
1902—H. L. Doherty
A. W. Gore
1903—H. L. Doherty
F. L. Riseley
1904—H. L. Doherty
F. L. Riseley
1905—H. L. Doherty
N. E. Brookes
1906—H. L. Doherty
F. L. Riseley
★1907—N. E. Brookes
A. W. Gore
★1908—A. W. Gore
H. Roper Barrett
1909—A. W. Gore
M. J. G. Ritchie
1910—A. F. Wilding
A. W. Gore

1911—A. F. Wilding
H. Roper Barrett
1912—A. F. Wilding
A. W. Gore
1913—A. F. Wilding
M. E. McLoughlin
1914—N. E. Brookes
A. F. Wilding
1919—G. L. Patterson
N. E. Brookes
1920—W. T. Tilden
G. L. Patterson
1921—W. T. Tilden
B. I. C. Norton
★†1922—G. L. Patterson
R. Lycett
1923—W. M. Johnston
F. T. Hunter
1924—J. Borotra
R. Lacoste
1925—R. Lacoste
J. Borotra
1926—J. Borotra
H. Kinsey
1927—H. Cochet
J. Borotra
1928—R. Lacoste
H. Cochet
1929—H. Cochet
J. Borotra
1930—W. T. Tilden
W. Allison
1931—S. B. Wood
F. X. Shields

1932—H. E. Vines
H. W. Austin
1933—J. H. Crawford
H. E. Vines
1934—F. J. Perry
J. H. Crawford
1935—F. J. Perry
G. von Cramm
1936—F. J. Perry
G. von Cramm
★1937—J. D. Budge
G. von Cramm
1938—J. D. Budge
H. W. Austin
★1939—R. L. Riggs
E. T. Cooke
★1946—Y. Petra
G. E. Brown
1947—J. Kramer
T. Brown
★1948—R. Falkenburg
J. E. Bromwich
1949—F. R. Schroeder
J. Drobny
★1950—B. Patty
F. A. Sedgman
1951—R. Savitt
K. McGregor
1952—F. A. Sedgman
J. Drobny
★1953—V. Seixas
K. Nielsen
1954—J. Drobny
K. R. Rosewall

1955—T. Trabert
K. Nielsen
★1956—L. A. Hoad
K. R. Rosewall
1957—L. A. Hoad
A. J. Cooper
★1958—A. J. Cooper
N. A. Fraser
★1959—A. Olmedo
R. Laver
★1960—N. A. Fraser
R. Laver
1961—R. Laver
C. R. McKinley
1962—R. Laver
M. F. Mulligan
★1963—C. R. McKinley
F. S. Stolle
1964—R. Emerson
F. S. Stolle
1965—R. Emerson
F. S. Stolle
1966—M. Santana
R. D. Ralston
1967—J. D. Newcombe
W. P. Bungert
1968—R. Laver
A. D. Roche
1969—R. Laver
J. D. Newcombe
1970—J. D. Newcombe
K. R. Rosewall
1971—J. D. Newcombe
S. R. Smith

★1972—S. R. Smith
I. Nastase
★1973—J. Kodes
A. Metrevtli
1974—J. S. Connors
K. R. Rosewall
1975—A. R. Ashe
J. S. Connors
1976—B. Borg
I. Nastase
1977—B. Borg
J. S. Connors
1978—B. Borg
J. S. Connors
1979—B. Borg
R. Tanner
1980—B. Borg
J. P. McEnroe
1981—J. P. McEnroe
B. Borg
1982—J. S. Connors
J. P. McEnroe
1983—J. P. McEnroe
C. J. Lewis
1984—J. P. McEnroe
J. S. Connors

MEN'S DOUBLES

1879—L. R. Erskine and H. F. Lawford
F. Durant and G. E. Tabor
1880—W. Renshaw and E. Renshaw
O. E. Woodhouse and C. J. Cole
1881—W. Renshaw and E. Renshaw
W. J. Down and H. Vaughan
1882—J. T. Hartley and R. T. Richardson
J. G. Horn and C. B. Russell
1883—C. W. Grinstead and C. E. Welldon
C. B. Russell and R. T. Milford
1884—W. Renshaw and E. Renshaw
E. W. Lewis and E. L. Williams
1885—W. Renshaw and E. Renshaw
C. E. Farrar and A. J. Stanley
1886—W. Renshaw and E. Renshaw
C. E. Farrar and A. J. Stanley
1887—P. Bowes-Lyon and H. W. W. Wilberforce
J. H. Crispe and Barratt Smith
1888—W. Renshaw and E. Renshaw
P. B. Lyon and H. W. W. Wilberforce
1889—W. Renshaw and E. Renshaw
E. W. Lewis and G. W. Hillyard
1890—J. Pim and F. O. Stoker
E. W. Lewis and G. W. Hillyard
1891—W. Baddeley and H. Baddeley
J. Pim and F. O. Stoker
1892—H. S. Barlow and E. W. Lewis
W. Baddeley and H. Baddeley
1893—J. Pim and F. O. Stoker
E. W. Lewis and H. S. Barlow
1894—W. Baddeley and H. Baddeley
H. S. Barlow and C. H. Martin
1895—W. Baddeley and H. Baddeley
E. W. Lewis and W. V. Eaves
1896—W. Baddeley and H. Baddeley
R. F. Doherty and H. A. Nisbet
1897—R. F. Doherty and H. L. Doherty
W. Baddeley and H. Baddeley
1898—R. F. Doherty and H. L. Doherty
H. A. Nisbet and C. Hobart
1899—R. F. Doherty and H. L. Doherty
H. A. Nisbet and C. Hobart
1900—R. F. Doherty and H. L. Doherty
H. Roper Barrett and H. A. Nisbet
1901—R. F. Doherty and H. L. Doherty
Dwight Davis and Holcombe Ward
1902—S. H. Smith and F. L. Riseley
R. F. Doherty and H. L. Doherty
1903—R. F. Doherty and H. L. Doherty
S. H. Smith and F. L. Riseley
1904—R. F. Doherty and H. L. Doherty
S. H. Smith and F. L. Riseley
1905—R. F. Doherty and H. L. Doherty
S. H. Smith and F. L. Riseley
1906—S. H. Smith and F. L. Riseley
R. F. Doherty and H. L. Doherty
1907—N. E. Brookes and A. F. Wilding
B. C. Wright and K. Behr
1908—A. F. Wilding and M. J. G. Ritchie
A. W. Gore and H. Roper Barrett
1909—A. W. Gore and H. Roper Barrett
S. N. Doust and H. A. Parker
1910—A. F. Wilding and M. J. G. Ritchie
A. W. Gore and H. Roper Barrett

1911—M. Decugis and A. H. Gobert
M. J. G. Ritchie and A. F. Wilding
1912—H. Roper Barrett and C. P. Dixon
M. Decugis and A. H. Gobert
1913—H. Roper Barrett and C. P. Dixon
F. W. Rahe and H. Kleinschroth
1914—N. E. Brookes and A. F. Wilding
H. Roper Barrett and C. P. Dixon
1919—R. V. Thomas and P. O'Hara-Wood
R. Lycett and R. W. Heath
1920—R. N. Williams and C. S. Garland
A. R. F. Kingscote and J. C. Parke
1921—R. Lycett and M. Woosnam
F. G. Lowe and A. H. Lowe
†1922—R. Lycett and J. O. Anderson
G. L. Patterson and P. O'Hara-Wood
1923—R. Lycett and L. A. Godfree
Count de Gomar and E. Flaquer
1924—F. T. Hunter and V. Richards
R. N. Williams and W. M. Washburn
1925—J. Borotra and R. Lacoste
J. Hennessey and R. Casey
1926—H. Cochet and J. Brugnon
V. Richards and H. Kinsey
1927—F. T. Hunter and W. T. Tilden
J. Brugnon and H. Cochet
1928—H. Cochet and J. Brugnon
G. L. Patterson and J. B. Hawkes
1929—W. Allison and J. Van Ryn
J. C. Gregory and I. G. Collins
1930—W. Allison and J. Van Ryn
J. H. Doeg and G. M. Lott
1931—G. M. Lott and J. Van Ryn
H. Cochet and J. Brugnon
1932—J. Borotra and J. Brugnon
G. P. Hughes and F. J. Perry
1933—J. Borotra and J. Brugnon
R. Nunoi and J. Satoh
1934—G. M. Lott and L. R. Stoefen
J. Borotra and J. Brugnon
1935—J. H. Crawford and A. K. Quist
W. Allison and J. Van Ryn
1936—G. P. Hughes and C. R. D. Tuckey
C. E. Hare and F. H. D. Wilde
1937—J. D. Budge and G. Mako
G. P. Hughes and C. R. D. Tuckey
1938—J. D. Budge and G. Mako
H. Henkel and G. von Metaxa
1939—R. L. Riggs and E. T. Cooke
C. E. Hare and F. H. D. Wilde
1946—T. Brown and J. Kramer
G. E. Brown and D. Pails
1947—R. Falkenburg and J. Kramer
A. J. Mottram and O. W. Sidwell
1948—J. E. Bromwich and F. A. Sedgman
T. Brown and G. Mulloy
1949—R. Gonzales and F. Parker
G. Mulloy and F. R. Schroeder
1950—J. E. Bromwich and A. K. Quist
G. E. Brown and O. W. Sidwell
1951—K. McGregor and F. A. Sedgman
J. Drobny and E. W. Sturgess
1952—K. McGregor and F. A. Sedgman
V. Seixas and E. W. Sturgess

1953—L. A. Hoad and K. R. Rosewall
R. N. Hartwig and M. G. Rose
1954—R. N. Hartwig and M. G. Rose
V. Seixas and T. Trabert
1955—R. N. Hartwig and L. A. Hoad
N. A. Fraser and K. R. Rosewall
1956—L. A. Hoad and K. R. Rosewall
N. Pietrangeli and O. Sirola
1957—G. Mulloy and B. Patty
N. A. Fraser and L. A. Hoad
1958—S. Davidson and U. Schmidt
A. J. Cooper and N. A. Fraser
1959—R. Emerson and N. A. Fraser
R. Laver and R. Mark
1960—R. H. Osuna and R. D. Ralston
M. G. Davies and R. K. Wilson
1961—R. Emerson and N. A. Fraser
R. A. J. Hewitt and F. S. Stolle
1962—R. A. J. Hewitt and F. S. Stolle
B. Jovanovic and N. Pilic
1963—R. H. Osuna and A. Palafox
J. C. Barclay and P. Darmon
1964—R. A. J. Hewitt and F. S. Stolle
R. Emerson and K. N. Fletcher
1965—J. D. Newcombe and A. D. Roche
K. N. Fletcher and R. A. J. Hewitt
1966—K. N. Fletcher and J. D. Newcombe
W. W. Bowrey and O. K. Davidson
1967—R. A. J. Hewitt and F. D. McMillan
R. Emerson and K. N. Fletcher
1968—J. D. Newcombe and A. D. Roche
K. R. Rosewall and F. S. Stolle
1969—J. D. Newcombe and A. D. Roche
T. S. Okker and M. C. Riessen
1970—J. D. Newcombe and A. D. Roche
K. R. Rosewall and F. S. Stolle
1971—R. S. Emerson and R. G. Laver
A. R. Ashe and R. D. Ralston
1972—R. A. J. Hewitt and F. D. McMillan
S. R. Smith and E. J. van Dillen
1973—J. S. Connors and I. Nastase
J. R. Cooper and N. A. Fraser
1974—J. D. Newcombe and A. D. Roche
R. C. Lutz and S. R. Smith
1975—V. Gerulaitis and A. Mayer
C. Dowdeswell and A. J. Stone
1976—B. E. Gottfried and R. Ramirez
R. L. Case and G. Masters
1977—R. L. Case and G. Masters
J. G. Alexander and P. C. Dent
1978—R. A. J. Hewitt and F. D. McMillan
P. Fleming and J. P. McEnroe
1979—P. Fleming and J. P. McEnroe
B. E. Gottfried and R. Ramirez
1980—P. McNamara and P. McNamee
R. C. Lutz and S. R. Smith
1981—P. Fleming and J. P. McEnroe
R. C. Lutz and S. R. Smith
1982—P. McNamara and P. McNamee
P. Fleming and J. P. McEnroe
1983—P. Fleming and J. P. McEnroe
T. E. Gullikson and T. R. Gullikson
1984—P. Fleming and J. P. McEnroe
P. Cash and P. McNamee

LADIES' SINGLES

1884—Miss M. Watson
Miss Watson

1885—Miss M. Watson
Miss B. Bingley

1886—Miss B. Bingley
Miss M. Watson

1887—Miss L. Dod
Miss B. Bingley

1888—Miss L. Dod
Mrs. G. W. Hillyard

★1889—Mrs. G. W. Hillyard
Miss L. Rice

★1890—Miss L. Rice
Miss Jacks

★1891—Miss L. Dod
Mrs. G. W. Hillyard

1892—Miss L. Dod
Mrs. G. W. Hillyard

1893—Miss L. Dod
Mrs. G. W. Hillyard

★1894—Mrs. G. W. Hillyard
Miss Austin

★1895—Miss C. Cooper
Miss Jackson

1896—Miss C. Cooper
Mrs. Pickering

1897—Mrs. G. W. Hillyard
Miss C. Cooper

★1898—Miss C. Cooper
Miss Martin

1899—Mrs. G. W. Hillyard
Miss C. Cooper

1900—Mrs. G. W. Hillyard
Miss C. Cooper

1901—Mrs. A. Sterry
Mrs. G. W. Hillyard

1902—Miss M. E. Robb
Mrs. A. Sterry

★1903—Miss D. K. Douglass
Miss E. W. Thomson

1904—Miss D. K. Douglass
Mrs. A. Sterry

1905—Miss M. Sutton
Miss D. K. Douglass

1906—Miss D. K. Douglass
Miss M. Sutton

1907—Miss M. Sutton
Mrs. Lambert Chambers

★1908—Mrs. A. Sterry
Miss A. M. Morton

★1909—Miss D. P. Boothby
Miss A. M. Morton

1910—Mrs. Lambert Chambers
Miss D. P. Boothby

1911—Mrs. Lambert Chambers
Miss D. P. Boothby

★1912—Mrs. D. R. Larcombe
Mrs. A. Sterry

★1913—Mrs. Lambert Chambers
Mrs. R. J. McNair

1914—Mrs. Lambert Chambers
Mrs. D. R. Larcombe

1919—Mlle. S. Lenglen
Mrs. Lambert Chambers

1920—Mlle S. Lenglen
Mrs. Lambert Chambers

1921—Mlle. S. Lenglen
Miss E. Ryan

†1922—Mlle. S. Lenglen
Mrs. Mallory

1923—Mlle. S. Lenglen
Miss K. McKane

1924—Miss K. McKane
Miss H. Wills

1925—Mlle. S. Lenglen
Miss J. Fry

1926—Miss L. A. Godfree
Sta. L. de Alvarez

1927—Miss H. Wills
Sta. L. de Alvarez

1928—Miss H. Wills
Sta. L. de Alvarez

1929—Miss H. Wills
Miss H. H. Jacobs

1930—Mrs. F. S. Moody
Miss E. Ryan

★1931—Fraulein C. Aussem
Fraulein H. Krahwinkel

1932—Mrs. F. S. Moody
Miss H. H. Jacobs

1933—Mrs. F. S. Moody
Miss D. E. Round

★1934—Miss D. E. Round
Miss H. H. Jacobs

1935—Mrs. F. S. Moody
Miss H. H. Jacobs

★1936—Miss H. H. Jacobs
Frau. S. Sperling

1937—Miss D. E. Round
Miss J. Jedrzejowska

★1938—Mrs. F. S. Moody
Miss H. H. Jacobs

★1939—Miss A. Marble
Miss K. E. Stammers

★1946—Miss P. Betz
Miss L. Brough

★1947—Miss M. Osborne
Miss D. Hart

1948—Miss L. Brough
Miss D. Hart

1949—Miss L. Brough
Mrs. W. du Pont

1950—Miss L. Brough
Mrs. W. du Pont

1951—Miss D. Hart
Miss S. Fry

1952—Miss M. Connolly
Miss L. Brough

1953—Miss M. Connolly
Miss D. Hart

1954—Miss M. Connolly
Miss L. Brough

★1955—Miss L. Brough
Mrs. J. Fleitz

1956—Miss S. Fry
Miss A. Buxton

★1957—Miss A. Gibson
Miss D. R. Hard

1958—Miss A. Gibson
Miss A. Mortimer

★1959—Miss M. E. Bueno
Miss D. R. Hard

1960—Miss M. E. Bueno
Miss S. Reynolds

★1961—Miss A. Mortimer
Miss C. C. Truman

1962—Mrs. J. R. Susman
Mrs. V. Sukova

★1963—Miss M. Smith
Miss B. J. Moffitt

1964—Miss M. E. Bueno
Miss M. Smith

1965—Miss M. Smith
Miss M. E. Bueno

1966—Mrs. L. W. King
Miss M. E. Bueno

1967—Mrs. L. W. King
Mrs. P. F. Jones

1968—Mrs. L. W. King
Miss J. A. M. Tegart

1969—Mrs. P. F. Jones
Mrs. L. W. King

★1970—Mrs. B. M. Court
Mrs. L. W. King

1971—Miss E. F. Goolagong
Mrs. B. M. Court

1972—Mrs. L. W. King
Miss E. F. Goolagong

1973—Mrs. L. W. King
Miss C. M. Evert

1974—Miss C. M. Evert
Mrs. O. Morozova

1975—Mrs. L. W. King
Mrs. R. Cawley

★1976—Miss C. M. Evert
Mrs. R. Cawley

1977—Miss S. V. Wade
Miss B. F. Stove

1978—Miss M. Navratilova
Miss C. M. Evert

1979—Miss M. Navratilova
Miss C. M. Evert

1980—Mrs. R. Cawley
Miss M. Navratilova

1981—Mrs. J. M. Lloyd
Miss H. Mandlikova

1982—Miss M. Navratilova
Mrs. J. M. Lloyd

1983—Miss M. Navratilova
Miss A. Jaeger

1984—Miss M. Navratilova
Mrs. J. M. Lloyd

LADIES' DOUBLES

1913—Mrs. R. J. McNair and Miss D. P. Boothby
Mrs. A. Sterry and Mrs. Lambert Chambers

1914—Miss E. Ryan and Miss A. M. Morton
Mrs. D. R. Larcombe and Mrs. Hannam

1919—Mlle. S. Lenglen and Miss E. Ryan
Mrs. Lambert Chambers and Mrs. D. R. Larcombe

1920—Mlle. S. Lenglen and Miss E. Ryan
Mrs. Lambert Chambers and Mrs. D. R. Larcombe

1921—Mlle. S. Lenglen and Miss E. Ryan
Mrs. A. E. Beamish and Mrs. Peacock

1922—Mlle. S. Lenglen and Miss E. Ryan
Mrs. A. D. Stocks and Miss K. McKane

1923—Mlle. S. Lenglen and Miss E. Ryan
Miss J. Austin and Miss E. L. Colyer

1924—Mrs. H. Wightman and Miss H. Wills
Mrs. B. C. Covell and Miss K. McKane

1925—Mlle. S. Lenglen and Miss E. Ryan
Mrs. A. V. Bridge and Miss C. G. McIlquham

1926—Miss E. Ryan and Miss M. K. Browne
Mrs. L. A. Godfree and Miss E. L. Colyer

1927—Miss H. Wills and Miss E. Ryan
Miss E. L. Heine and Mrs. Peacock

1928—Mrs. Holcroft-Watson and Miss P. Saunders
Miss E. H. Harvey and Miss E. Bennett

1929—Mrs. Holcroft-Watson and Mrs. L. R. C. Michell
Mrs. B. C. Covell and Mrs. D. C. Shepherd-Barron

1930—Mrs. F. S. Moody and Miss E. Ryan
Miss E. Cross and Miss S. Palfrey

1931—Mrs. D. C. Shepherd-Barron and Miss P. E. Mudford
Mlle. D. Metaxa and Mlle. J. Sigart

1932—Mlle. D. Metaxa and Mlle. J. Sigart
Miss E. Ryan and Miss H. H. Jacobs

1933—Mme. R. Mathieu and Miss E. Ryan
Miss F. James and Miss A. M. Yorke

1934—Mme. R. Mathieu and Miss E. Ryan
Mrs. D. Andrus and Mme. Henrotin

1935—Miss F. James and Miss K. E. Stammers
Mme. R. Mathieu and Frau. S. Sperling

1936—Miss F. James and Miss K. E. Stammers
Mrs. S. P. Fabyan and Miss H. H. Jacobs

1937—Mme. R. Mathieu and Miss A. M. Yorke
Mrs. M. R. King and Mrs. J. B. Pittman

1938—Mrs. S. P. Fabyan and Miss A. Marble
Mme. R. Mathieu and Miss A. M. Yorke

1939—Mrs. S. P. Fabyan and Miss A. Marble
Miss H. H. Jacobs and Miss A. M. Yorke

1946—Miss L. Brough and Miss M. Osborne
Miss P. Betz and Miss D. Hart

1947—Miss D. Hart and Miss P. C. Todd
Miss L. Brough and Miss M. Osborne

1948—Miss L. Brough and Mrs. W. du Pont
Miss D. Hart and Mrs. P. C. Todd

1949—Miss L. Brough and Mrs. W. du Pont
Miss G. Moran and Miss P. C. Todd

1950—Miss L. Brough and Mrs. W. du Pont
Miss S. Fry and Miss D. Hart

1951—Miss S. Fry and Miss D. Hart
Miss L. Brough and Mrs. W. du Pont

1952—Miss S. Fry and Miss D. Hart
Miss L. Brough and Miss M. Connolly

1953—Miss S. Fry and Miss D. Hart
Miss M. Connolly and Miss J. Sampson

1954—Miss L. Brough and Mrs. W. du Pont
Miss S. Fry and Miss D. Hart

1955—Miss A. Mortimer and Miss J. A. Shilcock
Miss J. Bloomer and Miss P. E. Ward

1956—Miss A. Buxton and Miss A. Gibson
Miss F. Muller and Miss D. G. Seeney

1957—Miss A. Gibson and Miss D. R. Hard
Miss K. Hawton and Miss T. D. Long

1958—Miss M. E. Bueno and Miss A. Gibson
Mrs. W. du Pont and Miss M. Varner

1959—Miss J. Arth and Miss D. R. Hard
Mrs. J. G. Fleitz and Miss C. C. Truman

1960—Miss M. E. Bueno and Miss D. R. Hard
Miss S. Reynolds and Miss R. Schuurman

1961—Miss K. Hantze and Miss B. J. Moffitt
Miss J. Lehane and Miss M. Smith

1962—Miss B. J. Moffitt and Mrs. J. R. Susman
Mrs. L. E. G. Price and Miss R. Schuurman

1963—Miss M. E. Bueno and Miss D. R. Hard
Miss R. A. Ebbern and Miss M. Smith

1964—Miss M. Smith and Miss L. R. Turner
Miss B. J. Moffitt and Mrs. J. R. Susman

1965—Miss M. E. Bueno and Miss B. J. Moffitt
Miss F. Durr and Miss J. Lieffrig

1966—Miss M. E. Bueno and Miss N. Richey
Miss M. Smith and Miss J. A. M. Tegart

1967—Miss R. Casals and Mrs. L. W. King
Miss M. E. Bueno and Miss N. Richey

1968—Miss R. Casals and Mrs. L. W. King
Miss F. Durr and Mrs. P. F. Jones

1969—Mrs. B. M. Court and Miss J. A. M. Tegart
Miss P. S. A. Hogan and Miss M. Michel

1970—Miss R. Casals and Mrs. L. W. King
Miss F. Durr and Miss S. V. Wade

1971—Miss R. Casals and Mrs. L. W. King
Mrs. B. M. Court and Miss E. F. Goolagong

1972—Mrs. L. W. King and Miss B. F. Stove
Mrs. D. E. Dalton and Miss F. Durr

1973—Miss R. Casals and Mrs. L. W. King
Miss F. Durr and Miss B. F. Stove

1974—Miss E. F. Goolagong and Miss M. Michel
Miss H. F. Gourlay and Miss K. M. Krantzcke

1975—Miss A. K. Kiyomura and Miss K. Sawamatsu
Miss F. Durr and Miss B. F. Stove

1976—Miss C. M. Evert and Miss M. Navratilova
Mrs. L. W. King and Miss B. F. Stove

1977—Mrs. H. F. Gourlay Cawley and Miss J. C. Russell
Miss M. Navratilova and Miss B. F. Stove

1978—Mrs. G. E. Reid and Miss W. M. Turnbull
Miss M. Jausovec and Miss V. Ruzici

1979—Mrs. L. W. King and Miss M. Navratilova
Miss B. F. Stove and Miss W. M. Turnbull

1980—Miss K. Jordan and Miss A. E. Smith
Miss R. Casals and Miss W. M. Turnbull

1981—Miss M. Navratilova and Miss P. H. Shriver
Miss K. Jordan and Miss A. E. Smith

1982—Miss M. Navratilova and Miss P. H. Shriver
Miss K. Jordan and Miss A. E. Smith

1983—Miss M. Navratilova and Miss P. H. Shriver
Miss R. Casals and Miss W. M. Turnbull

1984—Miss M. Navratilova and Miss P. H. Shriver
Miss K. Jordan and Miss A. E. Smith

NOTE.—*For the years 1913, 1914 and 1919-1923 inclusive the above records include the "World's Championship on Grass" granted to The Lawn Tennis Association by The International Lawn Tennis Federation. This title was then abolished and commencing in 1924 they became The Official Lawn Tennis Championships recognised by The International Lawn Tennis Federation.*

†*Challenge Round abolished: holders subsequently played through.*

Prior to 1922 the holders in the Singles Events and Gentlemen's Doubles did not compete in the Championships but met the winners of these events in the Challenge Rounds.

★*The holder did not defend the title.*

THE CHAMPIONSHIP ROLL

MIXED DOUBLES

1913—Hope Crisp and Mrs. C. O. Tuckey
J. C. Parke and Mrs. D. R. Larcombe
1914—J. C. Parke and Mrs. D. R. Larcombe
A. F. Wilding and Mlle. Broquedis
1919—R. Lycett and Miss E. Ryan
A. D. Prebble and Mrs. Lambert Chambers
1920—G. L. Patterson and Mlle. S. Lenglen
R. Lycett and Miss E. Ryan
1921—R. Lycett and Miss E. Ryan
M. Woosnam and Miss P. L. Howkins
1922—P. O'Hara-Wood and Mlle. S. Lenglen
R. Lycett and Miss E. Ryan
1923—R. Lycett and Miss E. Ryan
L. S. Deane and Mrs. D. C. Shepherd-Barron
1924—J. B. Gilbert and Miss K. McKane
L. A. Godfree and Mrs. D. C. Shepherd-Barron
1925—J. Borotra and Mlle. S. Lenglen
H. L. de Morpurgo and Miss E. Ryan
1926—L. A. Godfree and Mrs. L. A. Godfree
H. Kinsey and Miss M. K. Browne
1927—F. T. Hunter and Miss E. Ryan
L. A. Godfree and Mrs. L. A. Godfree
1928—P. D. B. Spence and Miss E. Ryan
J. Crawford and Miss D. Akhurst
1929—F. T. Hunter and Miss H. Wills
I. G. Collins and Miss J. Fry
1930—J. H. Crawford and Miss E. Ryan
D. Prenn and Fraulein H. Krahwinkel
1931—G. M. Lott and Mrs. L. A. Harper
I. G. Collins and Miss J. C. Ridley
1932—E. Maier and Miss E. Ryan
H. C. Hopman and Mlle. J. Sigart
1933—G. von Cramm and Fraulein H. Krahwinkel
N. G. Farquharson and Miss M. Heeley
1934—R. Miki and Miss D. E. Round
H. W. Austin and Mrs. D. C. Shepherd-Barron
1935—F. J. Perry and Miss D. E. Round
H. C. Hopman and Mrs. H. C. Hopman
1936—F. J. Perry and Miss D. E. Round
J. D. Budge and Mrs. S. P. Fabyan
1937—J. D. Budge and Miss A. Marble
Y. Petra and Mme. R. Mathieu

1938—J. D. Budge and Miss A. Marble
H. Henkel and Mrs. S. P. Fabyan
1939—R. L. Riggs and Miss A. Marble
F. H. D. Wilde and Miss N. B. Brown
1946—T. Brown and Miss L. Brough
G. E. Brown and Miss D. Bundy
1947—J. E. Bromwich and Miss L. Brough
C. F. Long and Mrs. N. M. Bolton
1948—J. E. Bromwich and Miss L.Brough
F. A. Sedgman and Miss D. Hart
1949—E. W. Sturgess and Mrs. S. P. Summers
J. E. Bromwich and Miss L. Brough
1950—E. W. Sturgess and Miss L. Brough
G. E. Brown and Mrs. P. C. Todd
1951—F. A. Sedgman and Miss D. Hart
M. G. Rose and Mrs. N. M. Bolton
1952—F. A. Sedgman and Miss D. Hart
E. Morea and Mrs. T. D. Long
1953—V. Seixas and Miss D. Hart
E. Morea and Miss S. Fry
1954—V. Seixas and Miss D. Hart
K. R. Rosewall and Mrs. W. du Pont
1955—V. Seixas and Miss D. Hart
E. Morea and Miss A. L. Brough
1956—V. Seixas and Miss S. Fry
G. Mulloy and Miss A. Gibson
1957—M. G. Rose and Miss D. R. Hard
N. A. Fraser and Miss A. Gibson
1958—R. N. Howe and Miss L. Coghlan
K. Nielsen and Miss A. Gibson
1959—R. Laver and Miss D. R. Hard
N. A. Fraser and Miss M. E. Bueno
1960—R. Laver and Miss D. R. Hard
R. N. Howe and Miss M. E. Bueno
1961—F. S. Stolle and Miss L. R. Turner
R. N. Howe and Miss E. Buding
1962—N. A. Fraser and Mrs. W. du Pont
R. D. Ralston and Miss A. S. Haydon
1963—K. N. Fletcher and Miss M. Smith
R. A. J. Hewitt and Miss D. R. Hard
1964—F. S. Stolle and Miss L. R. Turner
K. N. Fletcher and Miss M. Smith

1965—K. N. Fletcher and Miss M. Smith
A. D. Roche and Miss J. A. M. Tegart
1966—K. N. Fletcher and Miss M. Smith
R. D. Ralston and Mrs. L. W. King
1967—O. K. Davidson and Mrs. L. W. King
K. N. Fletcher and Miss M. E. Bueno
1968—K. N. Fletcher and Mrs. B. M. Court
A. Metreveli and Miss O. Morozova
1969—F. S. Stolle and Mrs. P. F. Jones
A. D. Roche and Miss J. A. M. Tegart
1970—I. Nastase and Miss R. Casals
A. Metreveli and Miss O. Morozova
1971—O. K. Davidson and Mrs. L. W. King
M. C. Riessen and Mrs. B. M. Court
1972—I. Nastase and Miss R. Casals
K. G. Warwick and Miss E. F. Goolagong
1973—O. K. Davidson and Mrs. L. W. King
R. Ramirez and Miss J. S. Newberry
1974—O. K. Davidson and Mrs. L. W. King
M. J. Farrell and Miss L. J. Charles
1975—M. C. Riessen and Mrs. B. M. Court
A. J. Stone and Miss B. F. Stove
1976—A. D. Roche and Miss F. Durr
R. L. Stockton and Miss R. Casals
1977—R. A. J. Hewitt and Miss G. R. Stevens
F. D. McMillan and Miss B. F. Stove
1978—F. D. McMillan and Miss B. F. Stove
R. O. Ruffels and Mrs. L. W. King
1979—R. A. J. Hewitt and Miss G. R. Stevens
F. D. McMillan and Miss B. F. Stove
1980—J. R. Austin and Miss T. Austin
M. R. Edmondson and Miss D. L. Fromholtz
1981—F. D. McMillan and Miss B. F. Stove
J. R. Austin and Miss T. Austin
1982—K. Curren and Miss A. E. Smith
J. M. Lloyd and Miss W. M. Turnbull
1983—J. M. Lloyd and Miss W. M. Turnbull
S. Denton and Mrs. L. W. King
1984—J. M. Lloyd and Miss W. M. Turnbull
S. Denton and Miss K. Jordan

THE JUNIOR CHAMPIONSHIP ROLL

BOYS' SINGLES

1948—S. Stockenberg (Sweden)
1949—S. Stockenberg (Sweden)
1950—J. A. T. Horn (G.B.)
1951—J. Kupferburger (S.A.)
1952—R. K. Wilson (G.B.)
1953—W. A. Knight (G.B.)
1954—R. Krishnan (India)
1955—M. P. Hann (G.B.)
1956—R. Holmberg (U.S.A.)
1957—J. I. Tattersall (G.B.)

1958—E. Buchholz (U.S.A.)
1959—T. Lejus (U.S.S.R.)
1960—A. R. Mandelstam (S.A.)
1961—C. E. Graebner (U.S.A.)
1962—S. Matthews (G.B.)
1963—N. Kalogeropoulos (Greece)
1964—I. El Shafei (U.A.R.)
1965—V. Korotkov (U.S.S.R.)
1966—V. Korotkov (U.S.S.R.)

1967—M. Orantes (Spain)
1968—J. G. Alexander (Australia)
1969—B. Bertram (S.A.)
1970—B. Bertram (S.A.)
1971—R. Kreiss (U.S.A.)
1972—B. Borg (Sweden)
1973—W. Martin (U.S.A.)
1974—W. Martin (U.S.A.)
1975—C. J. Lewis (N.Z.)

1976—H. Guenthardt (Switzerland)
1977—V. A. Winitsky (U.S.A.)
1978—I. Lendl (Czechoslovakia)
1979—R. Krishnan (India)
1980—T. Tulasne (France)
1981—M. W. Anger (U.S.A.)
1982—P. Cash (Australia)
1983—S. Edberg (Sweden)
1984—M. Kratzmann (Australia)

BOYS' DOUBLES

1982—P. Cash and J. Frawley   1983—M. Kratzmann and S. Youl   1984—R. Brown and R. Weiss

GIRLS' SINGLES

1948—Miss O. Miskova (Czechoslovakia)
1949—Miss C. Mercelis (Belgium)
1950—Miss L. Cornell (G.B.)
1951—Miss L. Cornell (G.B.)
1952—Miss ten Bosch (Netherlands)
1953—Miss D. Kilian (S.A.)
1954—Miss V. A. Pitt (G.B.)
1955—Miss S. M. Armstrong (G.B.)
1956—Miss A. S. Haydon (G.B.)
1957—Miss M. Arnold (U.S.A.)

1958—Miss S. M. Moore (U.S.A.)
1959—Miss J. Cross (S.A.)
1960—Miss K. Hantze (U.S.A.)
1961—Miss G. Baksheeva (U.S.S.R.)
1962—Miss G. Baksheeva (U.S.S.R.)
1963—Miss D. M. Salfati (France)
1964—Miss P. Bartkowicz (U.S.A.)
1965—Miss O. Morozova (U.S.S.R.)
1966—Miss B. Lindstrom (Finland)

1967—Miss J. Salome (Netherlands)
1968—Miss K. Pigeon (U.S.A.)
1969—Miss K. Sawamatsu (Japan)
1970—Miss S. Walsh (U.S.A.)
1971—Miss M. Kroschina (U.S.S.R.)
1972—Miss I. Kloss (S.A.)
1973—Miss A. Kiyomura (U.S.A.)
1974—Miss M Jausovec (Yugoslavia)
1975—Miss N. Y. Chmyreva (U.S.S.R.)

1976—Miss N. Y. Chmyreva (U.S.S.R.)
1977—Miss L. Antonoplis (U.S.A.)
1978—Miss T. Austin (U.S.A.)
1979—Miss M. L. Piatek (U.S.A.)
1980—Miss D. Freeman (Australia)
1981—Miss Z. Garrison (U.S.A.)
1982—Miss C. Tanvier (France)
1983—Miss P. Paradis (France)
1984—Miss A. N. Croft (G.B.)

GIRLS' DOUBLES

1982—Miss B. Herr and Miss P. Barg   1983—Miss P. Fendick and Miss P. Hy   1984—Miss C. Kuhlman and Miss S. Rehe

LIST OF COMPETITORS

LADIES

Acker, Miss S. L. (U.S.A.)
Allen, Miss L. E. (U.S.A.)
Amiach, Miss S. (France)
Anderholm, Miss C. (Sweden)
Antonoplis, Miss L. (U.S.A.)
Arraya, Miss L. (Peru)
Barg, Miss P. (U.S.A.)
Barker, Miss S. (Great Britain)
Bassett, Miss C. (Canada)
Benjamin, Miss C. (U.S.A.)
Blount, Miss R. L. (U.S.A.)
Bonder, Miss L. (U.S.A.)
Bramblett, Miss B. C. (U.S.A.)
Brasher, Miss K. J. (Great Britain)
Brown, Miss A. J. (Great Britain)
Brown, Miss M. L. (U.S.A.)
Budarova, Miss I. (Czechoslovakia)
Bunge, Miss B. (Monaco)
Burgin, Miss E. M. (U.S.A.)
Byrne, Miss J. (Australia)
Calleja, Miss M. C. (France)
Casale, Miss P. (U.S.A.)
Casals, Miss R. (U.S.A.)
Cecchini, Miss A. M. (Italy)
Cherneva, Miss S. (U.S.S.R.)
Collins, Miss S. L. (U.S.A.)
Copeland, Miss C. (U.S.A.)
Copeland, Miss K. T. (U.S.A.)
Croft, Miss A. N. (Great Britain)
Crowe, Miss H. A. (U.S.A.)
Cummings, Miss K. B. (U.S.A.)
Dalton, Mrs. D. E. (Australia)
Delhees-Jauch, Mrs. P. (Switzerland)
Drescher, Miss L. (Switzerland)
Durie, Miss J. M. (Great Britain)
Einy, Miss R. L. (Great Britain)
Eliseenko, Miss E. (U.S.S.R.)
Fairbank, Miss R. D. (South Africa)
Fernandez, Miss A. M. (U.S.A.)
Fernandez, Miss G. (Puerto Rico)
Foltz, Miss S. P. (U.S.A.)

Garrison, Miss Z. L. (U.S.A.)
Gerken, Miss B. (U.S.A.)
Golder, Miss J. S. (U.S.A.)
Goles, Miss S. (Yugoslavia)
Gomer, Miss S. L. (Great Britain)
Gracie, Miss L. C. (Great Britain)
Graf, Miss S. (Germany)
Gregory, Miss N. F. (Australia)
Gulley, Miss A. L. (Australia)
Hanika, Miss S. (Germany)
Henricksson, Miss A. B. (U.S.A.)
Herr, Miss B. (U.S.A.)
Herreman, Miss N. (France)
Hetherington, Miss J. M. (Canada)
Hobbs, Miss A. E. (Great Britain)
Holladay, Miss T. A. (U.S.A.)
Holton, Miss A. E. (U.S.A.)
Horvath, Miss E. K. (U.S.A.)
Huber, Miss P. (Austria)
Inoue, Miss E. (Japan)
Jausovec, Miss M. (Yugoslavia)
Jexell, Miss C. (Sweden)
Jolissaint, Miss C. (Switzerland)
Jones, Miss E. S. (Great Britain)
Jordan, Miss B. K. (U.S.A.)
Jordan, Miss K. (U.S.A.)
Karlsson, Miss C. (Sweden)
Kim, Miss G. M. (U.S.A.)
Kinney, Miss K. (U.S.A.)
Kiyomura-Hayashi, Mrs. D. M. (U.S.A.)
Klitch, Miss J. L. (U.S.A.)
Kloss, Miss I. S. (South Africa)
Kohde-Kilsch, Miss C. (Germany)
Kuczynska, Miss I. (Poland)
Leand, Miss A. C. (U.S.A.)
Leipus, Miss N. A. (Australia)
Leo, Miss S. J. (Australia)
Lindqvist, Miss C. (Sweden)
Lloyd, Mrs. J. M. (U.S.A.)
Louie, Miss M. (U.S.A.)
Louis, Miss J. (Great Britain)

Ludloff, Miss H. A. (U.S.A.)
Mair, Miss S. T. (Great Britain)
Maleeva, Miss M. (Bulgaria)
Mandlikova, Miss H. (Czechoslovakia)
Manset, Miss H. (U.S.A.)
Margolin, Miss S. A. (U.S.A.)
Mascarin, Miss S. E. (U.S.A.)
McNeil, Miss L. (U.S.A.)
Medrado, Miss P. S. (Brazil)
Mentz, Miss R. (South Africa)
Mesker, Miss M. A. (Netherlands)
Minter, Miss A. L. (Australia)
Minter, Miss E. A. (Australia)
Mochizuki, Mrs. H. A. (U.S.A.)
Monteiro, Miss C. C. (Brazil)
Mould, Miss B. A. (South Africa)
Moulton, Miss A. A. (U.S.A.)
Mundel, Miss J. A. (South Africa)
Nagelsen, Miss B. (U.S.A.)
Navratilova, Miss M. (U.S.A.)
Nelson, Miss V. L. (U.S.A.)
Newton, Miss C. J. (New Zealand)
Norton, Miss B. (U.S.A.)
Paradis, Miss P. (France)
Pelletier, Miss H. (Canada)
Perry, Miss B. M. (New Zealand)
Pfaff, Miss E. S. (Germany)
Phelps, Miss T. (U.S.A.)
Piatek, Miss M. L. (U.S.A.)
Potter, Miss B. C. (U.S.A.)
Purdy, Miss G. (U.S.A.)
Quinlan, Miss M. (U.S.A.)
Raschiatore, Miss F. (U.S.A.)
Reeves, Miss S. E. (Great Britain)
Reggi, Miss R. (Italy)
Remilton, Miss B. J. (Australia)
Reva, Miss N. (U.S.S.R.)
Reynolds, Miss C. S. (U.S.A.)
Rimes, Miss S. K. (U.S.A.)
Rinaldi, Miss K. (U.S.A.)
Romanov, Miss L. (Rumania)

Rush, Miss G. A. (U.S.A.)
Ruzici, Miss V. (Rumania)
Salmon, Miss J. A. (Great Britain)
Sands, Miss K. Y. (U.S.A.)
Sato, Miss N. (Japan)
Savchenko, Miss L. (U.S.S.R.)
Sayers, Miss E. M. (Australia)
Scheuer-Larsen, Miss T. (Denmark)
Shaefer, Mrs. L. A. (U.S.A.)
Shriver, Miss P. H. (U.S.A.)
Simmonds, Miss S. (Italy)
Skronska, Miss K. (Czechoslovakia)
Skuherska, Miss M. (Czechoslovakia)
Smith, Miss A. E. (U.S.A.)
Smith, Miss P. G. (U.S.A.)
Steinmetz, Miss K. A. (U.S.A.)
Stove, Miss B. F. (Netherlands)
Strachonova, Miss H. (Switzerland)
Suire, Miss C. (France)
Sukova, Miss H. (Czechoslovakia)
Tanvier, Miss C. (France)
Teeguarden, Miss P. A. (U.S.A.)
Temesvari, Miss A. (Hungary)
Torres, Miss M. Y. (U.S.A.)
Turnbull, Miss W. M. (Australia)
Uys, Miss R. (South Africa)
Vanier, Miss C. (France)
Van Nostrand, Miss M. (U.S.A.)
Vasquez, Miss P. (Peru)
Vermaak, Miss Y. (South Africa)
Wade, Miss S. V. (Great Britain)
Walpole, Miss S. A. (Great Britain)
Walsh, Miss S. A. (U.S.A.)
White, Miss A. H. (U.S.A.)
White, Miss R. M. (U.S.A.)
White, Miss W. E. (U.S.A.)
Whytcross, Miss P. J. (Australia)
Wright, Mrs. F. I. (U.S.A.)
Yanagi, Miss M. (Japan)
Yeargin, Miss N. S. (U.S.A.)

GENTLEMEN

Acuna, R. (Chile)
Alexander, J. G. (Australia)
Amaya, V. C. (U.S.A.)
Amritraj, A. (India)
Amritraj, V. (India)
Andrews, A. (U.S.A.)
Annacone, P. (U.S.A.)
Arias, J. (U.S.A.)
Arraya, P. (Peru)
Bale, S. M. (G.B.)
Ball, S. (Australia)
Barbosa, G. (Brazil)
Bates, M. J. (G.B.)
Becker, B. (Germany)
Beutel, H. D. (Germany)
Boileau, B. J. E. (Belgium)
Bourne, L. R. (U.S.A.)
Bradnam, C. (G.B.)
Cain, T. (U.S.A.)
Canter, J. (U.S.A.)
Cash, P. (Australia)
Colombo, S. (Italy)
Connors, J. S. (U.S.A.)
Cox, C. H. (U.S.A.)
Curren, K. (South Africa)
Davidson, O. K. (Australia)
Davis, M. (U.S.A.)
Davis, S. E. (U.S.A.)
Delatte, T. (U.S.A.)
Denton, S. (U.S.A.)
Depalmer, M. (U.S.A.)
Dibley, C. S. (Australia)
Dickson, M. (U.S.A.)
Dier, J. M. (G.B.)
Donnelly, G. (U.S.A.)
Doohan, P. (Australia)
Dowdeswell, C. (G.B.)
Doyle, M. N. (Ireland)
Drewett, B. D. (Australia)
Dunk, C. M. (U.S.A.)
Dyke, B. (Australia)
Edberg, S. (Sweden)
Edmondson, M. R. (Australia)
Edwards, E. (South Africa)
Estep, M. (U.S.A.)

Fancutt, M. T. (Australia)
Fancutt, T. C. (Australia)
Feaver, J. W. (G.B.)
Fibak, W. (Poland)
Fillol, J. (Chile)
Fitzgerald, J. B. (Australia)
Flach, K. (U.S.A.)
Fleming, P. (U.S.A.)
Forget, G. (France)
Freeman, M. (U.S.A.)
Fulwood, N. A. (G.B.)
Gehring, R. (Germany)
Gerulaitis, V. (U.S.A.)
Giammalva, A. (U.S.A.)
Gilbert, B. (U.S.A.)
Gitlin, D. (U.S.A.)
Glickstein, S. (Israel)
Gomez, A. (Ecuador)
Gonzalez, F. (Paraguay)
Gottfried, B. E. (U.S.A.)
Graham, D. (U.S.A.)
Grant, R. R. (Australia)
Guenthardt, H. P. (Switzerland)
Guenthardt, M. (Switzerland)
Gullikson, T. E. (U.S.A.)
Gullikson, T. R. (U.S.A.)
Gunnarsson, J. (Sweden)
Guntrip, M. W. C. (G.B.)
Gurfein, J. (U.S.A.)
Harmon, R. (U.S.A.)
Hlasek, J. (Switzerland)
Hocevar, A. (Brazil)
Hocevar, M. (Brazil)
Holmes, G. (U.S.A.)
Hooper, C. (U.S.A.)
Jarryd, A. (Sweden)
Johnstone, C. M. (Australia)
Kirmayr, C. (Brazil)
Kohlberg, A. (U.S.A.)
Korita, E. (U.S.A.)
Kratzmann, M. (Australia)
Kriek, J. C. (U.S.A.)
Krishnan, R. (India)
Kuharszky, Z. (Hungary)
Leach, M. (U.S.A.)

Lendl, I. (Czechoslovakia)
Levine, B. H. (South Africa)
Lewis, C. J. (New Zealand)
Lewis, R. A. (G.B.)
Lloyd, D. A. (G.B.)
Lloyd, J. M. (G.B.)
Lutz, R. C. (U.S.A.)
Mansdorf, A. (Israel)
Manson, B. (U.S.A.)
Masur, W. (Australia)
Maurer, A. (Germany)
Mayer, A. A. (U.S.A.)
Mayer, G. (U.S.A.)
Mayotte, T. S. (U.S.A.)
McCain, S. (U.S.A.)
McEnroe, J. P. (U.S.A.)
McEnroe, P. (U.S.A.)
McMillan, F. D. (South Africa)
McNamee, P. (Australia)
Mecir, M. (Czechoslovakia)
Meister, S. (U.S.A.)
Menon, S. (India)
Meyer, R. (U.S.A.)
Mezzadri, C. (Switzerland)
Michibata, G. (Canada)
Miller, C. A. (Australia)
Mitchell, M. (U.S.A.)
Mitton, B. M. (South Africa)
Moor, T. (U.S.A.)
Moore, R. J. (South Africa)
Mortensen, M. (Denmark)
Motta, C. (Brazil)
Mustard, D. G. C. (New Zealand)
Nelson, R. (U.S.A.)
Newcombe, J. D. (Australia)
Nystrom, J. (Sweden)
Ocleppo, G. (Italy)
Odizor, N. (Nigeria)
Ostoja, M. (Yugoslavia)
Panatta, C. (Italy)
Pate, D. (U.S.A.)
Perkiss, S. (Israel)
Pfister, H. (U.S.A.)
Purcell, M. (U.S.A.)
Ralston, R. D. (U.S.A.)

Rennert, P. (U.S.A.)
Riessen, M. C. (U.S.A.)
Roger-Vasselin, C. (France)
Sadri, J. (U.S.A.)
Sanchez, E. (Spain)
Saviano, N. (U.S.A.)
Scanlon, W. (U.S.A.)
Schapers, M. (Netherlands)
Schwaier, H. (Germany)
Seguso, R. (U.S.A.)
Shaw, S. M. (G.B.)
Shiras, L. (U.S.A.)
Shirato, H. (Japan)
Simonsson, S. (Sweden)
Simpson, R. J. (New Zealand)
Slozil, P. (Czechoslovakia)
Smid, T. (Czechoslovakia)
Smith, J. R. (G.B.)
Soares, J. (Brazil)
Stadler, R. (Switzerland)
Stefanki, L. (U.S.A.)
Stewart, S. E. (U.S.A.)
Stockton, R. L. (U.S.A.)
Strode, C. D. (U.S.A.)
Sundstrom, H. (Sweden)
Taroczy, B. (Hungary)
Tarr, D. (South Africa)
Taygan, F. (U.S.A.)
Teacher, B. (U.S.A.)
Testerman, B. (U.S.A.)
Turpin, J. (U.S.A.)
Van Patten, V. (U.S.A.)
Van Rensburg, C. (South Africa)
Van't Hof, R. (U.S.A.)
Visser, D. T. (South Africa)
Walts, B. (U.S.A.)
Warder, L. (U.S.A.)
Warwick, K. (Australia)
Westphal, M. (Germany)
Whitecross, G. (Australia)
Wilander, M. (Sweden)
Wilkison, T. (U.S.A.)
Willenborg, B. (U.S.A.)
Winitsky, V. (U.S.A.)
Wittus, C. J. (U.S.A.)
Youl, S. (Australia)

MAIDEN NAMES OF LADY COMPETITORS

Mrs. D. E. Dalton—Miss J. A. M. Tegart
Mrs. J. M. Lloyd—Miss C. M. Evert
Mrs. F. I. Wright—Miss J. S. Newberry
Mrs. P. Delhees-Jauch—Miss P. Delhees
Mrs. H. A. Mochizuki—Miss T. B. Watanabe
Mrs. D. M. Kiyomura-Hayashi—Miss A. K. Kiyomura
Mrs. L. A. Shaefer—Miss K. G. Jones

Event I.—THE GENTLEMEN'S SINGLES CHAMPIONSHIP

The Winner becomes the holder, for the year only, of the CHALLENGE CUP presented to the Club by KING GEORGE V, and also of the CHALLENGE CUP presented by The All England Lawn Tennis and Croquet Club. The First Prize is a piece of silver, known as "The Renshaw Cup" annually presented to the Club by the surviving members of the family of the late ERNEST and WILLIAM RENSHAW. The Winner receives silver replicas of the two Challenge Cups. A Silver Medal is presented to the Runner-up and a Bronze Medal to each defeated Semi-finalist.

FIRST ROUND

1	J. P. McEnroe ①	(U.S.A.)
2	P. McNamee	(A.)
3	E. Sanchez	(SP.)
4	R. Harmon	(U.S.A.)
5	W. Fibak	(POL.)
6	J. Hlasek	(SWZ.)
7	S. Youl	(A.)
8	W. Masur	(A.)
9	B. Willenborg	(U.S.A.)
10	B. Becker	(G.)
11	J. Turpin	(U.S.A.)
12	N. Odizor	(NI.)
13	M. Freeman	(U.S.A.)
14	S. Perkiss	(ISR.)
15	E. Korita	(U.S.A.)
16	W. Scanlon ⑭	(U.S.A.)
17	V. Gerulaitis ⑮	(U.S.A.)
18	A. Giammalva	(U.S.A.)
19	B. Taroczy	(HU.)
20	R. A. Lewis	(G.B.)
21	E. Edwards	(S.A.)
22	C. Hooper	(U.S.A.)
23	P. Fleming	(U.S.A.)
24	B. Gilbert	(U.S.A.)
25	J. Gunnarsson	(SW.)
26	J. Sadri	(U.S.A.)
27	P. Arraya	(PE.)
28	M. Leach	(U.S.A.)
29	R. Acuna	(CH.)
30	J. Soares	(BR.)
31	C. A. Miller	(A.)
32	C. Mezzadri	(SWZ.)
33	M. Wilander ④	(SW.)
34	S. E. Stewart	(U.S.A.)
35	P. Cash	(A.)
36	R. Seguso	(U.S.A.)
37	J. B. Fitzgerald	(A.)
38	D. Pate	(U.S.A.)
39	M. J. Bates	(G.B.)
40	C. Motta	(BR.)
41	S. Colombo	(IT.)
42	R. Krishnan	(IN.)
43	R. Stadler	(SWZ.)
44	C. J. Lewis	(N.Z.)
45	B. Testerman	(U.S.A.)
46	C. Dowdeswell	(G.B.)
47	S. Denton	(U.S.A.)
48	K. Curren ⑪	(S.A.)
49	H. Sundstrom ⑨	(SW.)
50	B. J. E. Boileau	(B.)
51	M. R. Edmondson	(A.)
52	M. Purcell	(U.S.A.)
53	K. Flach	(U.S.A.)
54	R. Van't Hof	(U.S.A.)
55	V. Van Patten	(U.S.A.)
56	T. Moor	(U.S.A.)
57	B. Teacher	(U.S.A.)
58	G. Michibata	(C.)
59	H. P. Guenthardt	(SWZ.)
60	G. Forget	(F.)
61	S. M. Shaw	(G.B.)
62	C. Panatta	(IT.)
63	M. Mitchell	(U.S.A.)
64	A. Gomez ⑥	(EC.)
65	P. Annacone	(U.S.A.)
66	J. R. Smith	(G.B.)
67	C. Kirmayr	(BR.)
68	M. Dickson	(U.S.A.)
69	C. Van Rensburg	(S.A.)
70	M. Ostoja	(YU.)
71	M. N. Doyle	(IRE.)
72	A. A. Mayer	(U.S.A.)
73	H. Schwaier	(G.)
74	V. Amritraj	(IN.)
75	S. Meister	(U.S.A.)
76	H. D. Beutel	(G.)
77	B. D. Drewett	(A.)
78	S. Edberg	(SW.)
79	M. Westphal	(G.)
80	J. C. Kriek ⑫	(U.S.A.)
81	T. S. Mayotte ⑯	(U.S.A.)
82	M. Hocevar	(BR.)
83	F. Gonzalez	(PAR.)
84	B. E. Gottfried	(U.S.A.)
85	R. J. Simpson	(N.Z.)
86	T. E. Gullikson	(U.S.A.)
87	M. Schapers	(NTH.)
88	L. Shiras	(U.S.A.)
89	M. Davis	(U.S.A.)
90	B. Manson	(U.S.A.)
91	C. H. Cox	(U.S.A.)
92	C. J. Wittus	(U.S.A.)
93	S. Simonsson	(SW.)
94	S. Glickstein	(ISR.)
95	L. R. Bourne	(U.S.A.)
96	J. S. Connors ③	(U.S.A.)
97	J. Arias ⑤	(U.S.A.)
98	B. M. Mitton	(S.A.)
99	V. Winitsky	(U.S.A.)
100	G. Ocleppo	(IT.)
101	T. Cain	(U.S.A.)
102	M. Mecir	(CZ.)
103	J. Gurfein	(U.S.A.)
104	D. T. Visser	(S.A.)
105	S. M. Bale	(G.B.)
106	J. G. Alexander	(A.)
107	H. Pfister	(U.S.A.)
108	T. R. Gullikson	(U.S.A.)
109	M. Kratzmann	(A.)
110	N. A. Fulwood	(G.B.)
111	L. Stefanki	(U.S.A.)
112	T. Smid ⑬	(CZ.)
113	A. Jarryd ⑩	(SW.)
114	S. E. Davis	(U.S.A.)
115	J. Nystrom	(SW.)
116	T. Wilkison	(U.S.A.)
117	G. Holmes	(U.S.A.)
118	J. W. Feaver	(G.B.)
119	J. M. Lloyd	(G.B.)
120	A. Maurer	(G.)
121	R. Gehring	(G.)
122	P. Slozil	(CZ.)
123	G. Mayer	(U.S.A.)
124	Z. Kuharszky	(HU.)
125	D. Tarr	(S.A.)
126	C. Roger-Vasselin	(F.)
127	R. L. Stockton	(U.S.A.)
128	I. Lendl ②	(CZ.)

SECOND ROUND

- J. P. McEnroe ① — 6-4, 6-4, 6-7, 6-1
- R. Harmon — 7-6, 6-3, 3-4, 6-5, 7-6-3
- J. Hlasek — 7-5, 4-6, 6-2, 6-1
- W. Masur — 6-4, 4-6, 6-4, 4-6, 6-3
- B. Becker — 6-0, 6-0, 6-4
- N. Odizor — 6-2, 7-5, 7-6
- S. Perkiss — 6-3, 4-6, 6-1, 1-7
- W. Scanlon ⑭ — 7-6, 6-7, 6-2, 3-6, 13-11
- V. Gerulaitis ⑮ — 3-6, 6-1, 6-4, 6-7, 7-5
- B. Taroczy — 6-4, 4-6, 6-4, 7-6
- E. Edwards — 7-6, 3-6, 6-1, 6-3
- B. Gilbert — 4-6, 4-6, 6-4, 6-2, 6-3
- J. Sadri — 6-3, 6-7, 6-2, 6-3
- M. Leach — 7-6, 6-3, 6-7, 6-4
- R. Acuna — 7-6, 1-6, 4-6, 6-4, 6-4
- C. A. Miller — 6-3, 3-6, 6-3, 6-4
- M. Wilander ④ — 6-4, 6-4, 6-7, 7-5
- P. Cash — 7-6, 6-4, 6-4
- J. B. Fitzgerald — 6-3, 6-4, 6-4
- C. Motta — 6-3, 6-3, 6-1
- R. Krishnan — 4-6, 6-2, 7-6, 6-4
- C. J. Lewis — 6-3, 6-2, 6-2
- B. Testerman — 6-4, 6-3, 6-3
- K. Curren ⑪ — 6-4, 3-6, 4-6, 7-6, 6-4
- H. Sundstrom — 6-4, 7-6, 7-5
- M. R. Edmondson — 6-4, 6-4, 6-4
- K. Flach — 2-6, 6-4, 7-6, 6-3
- T. Moor — 4-6, 6-3, 6-2, 6-2
- G. Michibata — 7-6, 2-6, 6-3, 2-6, 6-4
- G. Forget — 6-2, 6-0, 6-3
- S. M. Shaw — 6-4, 6-2, 6-3
- A. Gomez ⑥ — 3-6, 7-6, 6-1, 7-6
- P. Annacone — 7-6, 6-3, 6-4
- M. Dickson — 4-6, 7-6, 3-6, 6-2, 6-3
- C. Van Rensburg — 6-2, 6-2, 6-3
- M. N. Doyle — 3-6, 7-5, 6-4, 6-7, 7-5
- H. Schwaier — 6-3, 6-4, 6-2
- S. Meister — 6-2, 3-6, 7-6, 7-5
- S. Edberg — 6-4, 3-6, 7-6, 6-2
- J. C. Kriek ⑫ — 6-3, 6-0, 2-6, 6-2, 6-4
- T. S. Mayotte ⑯ — 7-5, 7-6, 6-1
- F. Gonzalez — 6-2, 1-6, 6-2, 6-7, 6-2
- T. E. Gullikson — 7-6, 4-6, 6-7, 6-1, 6-2
- L. Shiras — 6-2, 6-7, 7-6, 7-6
- M. Davis — 6-3, 7-6, 6-3
- C. J. Wittus — 4-6, 4-6, 3-5-7, 2-6, 6-4
- S. Simonsson — 4-6, 6-2, 3-6, 6-3, 6-4
- J. S. Connors ③ — 7-5, 7-5, 6-2
- J. Arias ⑤ — 3-6, 6-3, 6-2
- G. Ocleppo — 6-4, 6-3, 4-6, 6-0
- M. Mecir — 6-3, 4-3, retired
- D. T. Visser — 6-2, 6-4, 6-1
- S. M. Bale — 7-6, 3-6, 4-6, 7-6, 6-2
- T. R. Gullikson — 6-3, 6-4, 5-7, 6-2
- M. Kratzmann — 6-7, 6-4, 6-2, 6-1
- T. Smid ⑬ — 6-4, 6-7, 0-6, 6-4, 6-2
- S. E. Davis — 4-6, 6-4, 6-3, 6-2
- J. Nystrom — 5-7, 7-6, 6-4, 7-5
- G. Holmes — 6-1, 6-3, 6-7, 6-2
- J. M. Lloyd — 3-6, 6-3, 3-6, 6-4, 6-3
- R. Gehring — 6-4, 6-7, 7-5, 6-2
- Z. Kuharszky — 7-6, 6-2, 4-6, 1-6, 8-6
- D. Tarr — 6-4, 1-6, 6-2, 6-1
- I. Lendl ② — 4-6, 6-0, 6-3, 5-7, 6-4

THIRD ROUND

- J. P. McEnroe ① — 6-1, 6-3, 7-5
- W. Masur — 6-4, 6-2, 7-5
- B. Becker — 6-3, 6-4, 4-2, ret'd
- W. Scanlon ⑭ — 6-2, 6-3, 6-3
- V. Gerulaitis ⑮ — 6-3, 7-5, 4-6, 6-4
- B. Gilbert — 6-3, 7-6, 3-6, 4-6, 8-6
- J. Sadri — 7-6, 3-6, 6-4, 6-4
- R. Acuna — 3-6, 6-3, 6-2, 6-4
- P. Cash — 6-7, 6-4, 6-2, 6-4
- C. Motta — 7-6, 4-6, 6-4, 6-1
- R. Krishnan — 6-3, 6-3, 6-3
- K. Curren ⑪ — 7-6, 6-1, 4-6, 6-2
- M. R. Edmondson — 6-7, 7-6, 6-4, 6-7, 8-6
- T. Moor — 6-4, 7-5, 6-2
- G. Forget — 7-6, 6-3, 6-4
- A. Gomez ⑥ — 7-6, 7-6, 6-2
- P. Annacone — 7-6, 7-6, 3-6, 6-1
- C. Van Rensburg — 4-6, 6-2, 7-5, 7-6
- S. Meister — 6-1, 6-3, 7-5
- J. C. Kriek ⑫ — 4-6, 6-7, 6-4, 6-1, 6-1
- T. S. Mayotte ⑯ — 7-5, 7-6, 7-6
- T. E. Gullikson — 3-6, 6-3, 6-4, 6-4
- M. Davis — 6-3, 6-4, 6-3
- J. S. Connors ③ — 6-2, 6-1, 6-3
- J. Arias ⑤ — 7-5, 5-7, 3-6, 7-6, 6-1
- D. T. Visser — 6-3, 6-2, 6-4
- T. R. Gullikson — 7-5, 6-3, 6-4
- T. Smid ⑬ — 6-3, 2-6, 6-7, 7-6, 8-6
- S. E. Davis — 6-1, 7-5, 6-7, 6-1
- J. M. Lloyd — 4-6, 6-3, 6-4, 6-1
- R. Gehring — 7-6, 7-5, 6-3
- I. Lendl ② — 6-3, 6-1, 6-3

FOURTH ROUND

- J. P. McEnroe ① — 6-0, 6-4, 6-3
- W. Scanlon ⑭ — 6-2, 2-6, 7-6, 1-2 ret'd
- V. Gerulaitis ⑮ — 7-6, 6-1, 3-6, 6-4
- J. Sadri — 7-5, 7-6, 7-5
- P. Cash — 6-1, 6-2, 6-4
- K. Curren ⑪ — 6-2, 3-6, 7-6, 7-6
- T. Moor — 6-3, 6-4, 3-6, 4-6, 6-2
- A. Gomez ⑥ — 6-3, 6-4, 4-6, 1-6, 9-7
- P. Annacone — 6-3, 4-6, 6-4, 6-2
- J. C. Kriek ⑫ — 6-2, 5-7, 6-4, 6-1
- T. S. Mayotte ⑯ — 6-4, 6-3, 6-4
- J. S. Connors ③ — 6-4, 6-3, 6-4
- J. Arias ⑤ — 5-7, 6-3, 7-6, 6-1
- T. Smid ⑬ — 7-5, 6-4, 6-3
- S. E. Davis — 6-4, 6-4, 7-6
- I. Lendl ② — 6-4, 6-2, 7-6

QUARTER-FINALS

- J. P. McEnroe ① — 6-3, 6-3, 6-1
- J. Sadri — 6-3, 7-5, 6-7, 4-6, 6-3
- P. Cash — 4-6, 6-2, 7-6, 6-1
- A. Gomez ⑥ — 6-0, 6-1, 7-6
- P. Annacone — 6-3, 6-2, 6-4
- J. S. Connors ③ — 6-7, 6-2, 6-0, 6-2
- T. Smid ⑬ — 7-5, 6-4, 6-3
- I. Lendl ② — 4-6, 6-4, 6-4, 5-7, 7-5

SEMI-FINALS

- J. P. McEnroe ① — 6-3, 6-3, 6-1
- P. Cash — 6-4, 6-4, 6-7, 7-6
- J. S. Connors ③ — 6-2, 6-4, 6-2
- I. Lendl ② — 6-1, 7-6, 6-3

- J. P. McEnroe ① — 6-3, 7-6, 6-4
- J. S. Connors ③ — 6-7, 6-3, 7-5, 6-1

FINAL

J. P. McEnroe ① — 6-1, 6-1, 6-2

Heavy type denotes seeded players. The encircled figure against names denotes the order in which they have been seeded.

150

Event II.—THE GENTLEMEN'S DOUBLES CHAMPIONSHIP

The Winners become the holders, for the year only, of the CHALLENGE CUPS, presented by the OXFORD UNIVERSITY LAWN TENNIS CLUB and the late SIR HERBERT WILBERFORCE respectively. The Winners receive silver replicas of the Challenge Cups. A Silver Medal is presented to each of the Runners-up, and a Bronze Medal to each defeated Semi-finalist.

FIRST ROUND

1　P. Fleming and J. P. McEnroe ①
2　S. Menon and G. Michibata
3　D. Gitlin and C. Hooper
4　J. Fillol and F. Gonzalez
5　T. C. Fancutt and M. Schapers
6　V. C. Amaya and H. Pfister
7　M. Purcell and V. Van Patten
8　A. Giammalva and S. Meister ⑬
9　J. G. Alexander and J. B. Fitzgerald ⑫
10　M. J. Bates and J. M. Dier
11　C. H. Cox and J. Hlasek
12　M. N. Doyle and A. Maurer
13　E. Edwards and D. T. Visser
14　D. Graham and L. Warder
15　B. Becker and W. Fibak
16　P. Slozil and T. Smid ⑥
17　K. Curren and S. Denton ④
18　G. Donnelly and C. J. Wittus
19　M. Davis and C. M. Dunk
20　J. Nystrom and M. Wilander
21　S. M. Bale and R. A. Lewis
22　R. Nelson and H. Shirato
23　M. Kratzmann and S. Youl
24　S. Edberg and A. Jarryd ⑨
25　C. Dowdeswell and V. Winitsky ⑮
26　T. Delatte and J. C. Kriek
27　B. E. Gottfried and M. Leach
28　L. Stefanki and R. Van't Hof
29　A. Mansdorf and S. Perkiss
30　J. M. Lloyd and R. L. Stockton
31　T. Cain and P. McEnroe
32　A. A. Mayer and F. Taygan ⑦
33　C. Kirmayr and C. Motta ⑧
34　P. Annacone and M. Depalmer
35　P. Doohan and M. T. Fancutt
36　J. W. Feaver and J. R. Smith
37　B. D. Drewett and K. Warwick
38　S. McCain and B. Willenborg
39　A. Amritraj and V. Amritraj
40　B. Dyke and W. Masur ⑭
41　B. M. Mitton and B. Walts ⑪
42　C. J. Lewis and T. Wilkison
43　A. Kohlberg and R. Meyer
44　A. Hocevar and M. Hocevar
45　C. D. Strode and J. C. Turpin
46　S. E. Davis and B. Teacher
47　P. Arraya and A. Gomez
48　T. E. Gullikson and T. R. Gullikson ③
49　P. Cash and P. McNamee ⑤
50　A. Andrews and J. Sadri
51　S. Simonsson and H. Sundstrom
52　J. Canter and D. Tarr
53　C. A. Miller and M. Mitchell
54　M. Guenthardt and Z. Kuharszky
55　J. Gunnarsson and M. Mortensen
56　K. Flach and R. Seguso ⑯
57　H. P. Guenthardt and B. Taroczy ⑩
58　C. Panatta and N. Saviano
59　C. Bradnam and S. M. Shaw
60　S. Colombo and G. Ocleppo
61　L. R. Bourne and M. Dickson
62　G. Barbosa and J. Soares
63　D. G. C. Mustard and R. J. Simpson
64　M. R. Edmondson and S. E. Stewart ②

SECOND ROUND

P. Fleming and J. P. McEnroe ① — 6-3, 6-3, 4-6, 6-3
D. Gitlin and C. Hooper — 4-6, 6-3, 3-6, 6-3, 11-9
T. C. Fancutt and M. Schapers — 3-6, 7-6, 7-6, 6-2
M. Purcell and V. Van Patten — 6-1, 6-4, 6-4
J. G. Alexander and J. B. Fitzgerald ⑫ — 7-6, 6-4, 6-4
C. H. Cox and J. Hlasek — 7-6, 6-4, 4-6, 6-4
E. Edwards and D. T. Visser — 6-3, 6-4, 6-2
P. Slozil and T. Smid ⑥ — 3-6, 3-6, 6-4, 6-1, 6-4
K. Curren and S. Denton ④ — 7-6, 6-3, 7-6
J. Nystrom and M. Wilander — 6-1, 6-2, 6-4
S. M. Bale and R. A. Lewis — 6-7, 6-3, 6-3, 7-6
S. Edberg and A. Jarryd — 6-4, 6-2, 6-3
T. Delatte and J. C. Kriek — 2-6, 6-4, 7-6, 6-3
L. Stefanki and R. Van't Hof — 6-2, 7-6, 6-4
J. M. Lloyd and R. L. Stockton — 6-2, 6-3, 6-3
A. A. Mayer and F. Taygan ⑦ — 6-3, 3-6, 6-1, 6-2
P. Annacone and M. Depalmer — 6-3, 6-4, 6-2
P. Doohan and M. T. Fancutt — 6-4, 7-6, 6-7, 6-4
B. D. Drewett and K. Warwick — 7-5, 6-7, 5-7, 7-6, 6-3
B. Dyke and W. Masur ⑭ — 6-4, 6-0, 6-2
C. J. Lewis and T. Wilkison — 7-5, 6-4, 6-4
A. Kohlberg and R. Meyer — 6-4, 6-4, 7-5
S. E. Davis and B. Teacher — 7-5, 6-3, 6-4
T. E. Gullikson and T. R. Gullikson ③ — 7-5, 6-4, 3-6, 6-4
P. Cash and P. McNamee ⑤ — 6-7, 6-3, 7-6, 6-3
S. Simonsson and H. Sundstrom — 6-4, 6-7, 2-6, 6-4, 6-4
C. A. Miller and M. Mitchell — 6-3, 7-6, 6-2
K. Flach and R. Seguso ⑯ — 6-4, 6-7, 7-5, 7-6
H. P. Guenthardt and B. Taroczy ⑩ — 6-4, 6-7, 6-2, 7-5
C. Bradnam and S. M. Shaw — 7-6, 3-6, 7-6, 6-4
L. R. Bourne and M. Dickson — 4-6, 7-6, 6-1, 7-6
M. R. Edmondson and S. E. Stewart ② — 6-7, 6-4, 5-7, 6-2, 6-4

THIRD ROUND

P. Fleming and J. P. McEnroe ① — 6-4, 6-4, 7-6
M. Purcell and V. Van Patten — 7-6, 6-4, 7-6
J. G. Alexander and J. B. Fitzgerald ⑫ — 7-6, 6-4, 7-6
P. Slozil and T. Smid ⑥ — 6-4, 6-2, 7-6
K. Curren and S. Denton ④ — 6-1, 6-4, 4-6, 6-7, 6-3
S. Edberg and A. Jarryd ⑨ — 6-4, 6-2, 6-4
T. Delatte and J. C. Kriek — 6-3, 7-5, 7-5
A. A. Mayer and F. Taygan ⑦ — 7-6, 7-6, 5-7, 7-5
P. Doohan and M. T. Fancutt — 6-4, 6-4, 6-4
B. Dyke and W. Masur ⑭ — 6-4, 1-6, 6-3, 7-6
C. J. Lewis and T. Wilkison — 7-6, 6-7, 6-4, 6-4
T. E. Gullikson and T. R. Gullikson ③ — 7-6, 7-6, 7-6
P. Cash and P. McNamee ⑤ — 4-6, 6-3, 6-7, 6-3, 6-4
K. Flach and R. Seguso ⑯ — 3-6, 7-6, 6-2, 6-2
H. P. Guenthardt and B. Taroczy ⑩ — 6-4, 4-6, 6-4, 7-6
M. R. Edmondson and S. E. Stewart ② — 7-5, 6-2, 6-2

QUARTER-FINALS

P. Fleming and J. P. McEnroe ① — 7-6, 6-1, 7-5
J. G. Alexander and J. B. Fitzgerald ⑫ — 7-6, 3-6, 7-6, 6-4
K. Curren and S. Denton ④ — 6-3, 6-7, 7-6, 6-4
A. A. Mayer and F. Taygan ⑦ — 7-6, 7-6, 5-7, 7-5
P. Doohan and M. T. Fancutt — 7-5, 6-4, 7-6
T. E. Gullikson and T. R. Gullikson ③ — 2-6, 7-6, 6-4, 6-4
P. Cash and P. McNamee ⑤ — 6-7, 6-7, 6-4, 6-4, 7-5
M. R. Edmondson and S. E. Stewart ② — 4-6, 7-6, 3-6, 6-3, 6-3

SEMI-FINALS

P. Fleming and J. P. McEnroe ① — 6-4, 6-4, 4-6, 6-4
A. A. Mayer and F. Taygan ⑦ — 7-6, 6-4, 6-4
P. Doohan and M. T. Fancutt — 0-6, 6-4, 3-6, 6-2, 6-3
P. Cash and P. McNamee ⑤ — 6-3, 3-6, 4-6, 7-5, 13-11

P. Fleming and J. P. McEnroe ① — 7-6, 7-6, 6-4
P. Cash and P. McNamee ⑤ — 6-1, 3-6, 3-6, 6-7, 7-5

FINAL

P. Fleming and J. P. McEnroe ① — 6-2, 5-7, 6-2, 3-6, 6-3

Heavy type denotes seeded players. The encircled figure against names denotes the order in which they have been seeded.

Event III.—THE LADIES' SINGLES CHAMPIONSHIP

The Winner becomes the holder, for the year only, of the CHALLENGE TROPHY presented by The All England Lawn Tennis and Croquet Club. The Winner receives a silver replica of the Trophy. A Silver Medal is presented to the Runner-up and a Bronze Medal to each defeated Semi-finalist.

	FIRST ROUND	SECOND ROUND	THIRD ROUND	FOURTH ROUND	QUARTER-FINALS	SEMI-FINALS	FINAL

FIRST ROUND

1 Miss M. Navratilova ① .. (U.S.A.)
2 Miss M. Louie .... (U.S.A.)
3 Miss S. T. Mair .... (G.B.)
4 Miss A. E. Holton .... (U.S.A.)
5 Miss T. Scheuer-Larsen ... (D.)
6 Miss A. A. Moulton ...... (U.S.A.)
7 Miss M. A. Mesker .... (NTH.)
8 Miss I. Budarova .... (CZ.)
9 Miss G. A. Rush .... (U.S.A.)
10 Miss B. Herr .... (U.S.A.)
11 Miss R. M. White .... (U.S.A.)
12 Miss E. M. Sayers .... (A.)
13 Miss B. Gerken .... (U.S.A.)
14 Miss C. Vanier .... (F.)
15 Miss J. Louis .... (G.B.)
16 Miss L. Bonder ⑪ .... (U.S.A.)
17 Miss C. Bassett ⑥ .... (C.)
18 Miss S. A. Walsh .... (U.S.A.)
19 Miss N. Herreman .... (F.)
20 Miss M. C. Calleja .... (F.)
21 Miss M. L. Piatek .... (U.S.A.)
22 Miss S. Hanika .... (G.)
23 Miss A. E. Hobbs .... (G.B.)
24 Miss C. S. Reynolds ...... (U.S.A.)
25 Miss J. L. Klitch .... (U.S.A.)
26 Miss S. L. Collins .... (U.S.A.)
27 Miss Y. Vermaak .... (S.A.)
28 Miss P. G. Smith .... (U.S.A.)
29 Miss N. Reva .... (U.S.S.R.)
30 Miss P. Paradis .... (F.)
31 Miss J. A. Mundel .... (S.A.)
32 Miss M. Maleeva ⑦ ...... (BUL.)
33 Miss P. H. Shriver ④ .... (U.S.A.)
34 Miss E. S. Pfaff .... (G.)
35 Miss G. Fernandez .... (P.R.)
36 Miss L. Drescher .... (SWZ.)
37 Miss W. E. White .... (U.S.A.)
38 Miss M. Jausovec .... (YU.)
39 Miss A. C. Leand .... (U.S.A.)
40 Miss C. Benjamin .... (U.S.A.)
41 Miss M. L. Brown .... (U.S.A.)
42 Miss R. Uys .... (S.A.)
43 Miss L. Savchenko .... (U.S.S.R.)
44 Miss M. Skuherska .... (CZ.)
45 Miss G. M. Kim .... (U.S.A.)
46 Miss E. Inoue .... (J.)
47 Miss C. Suire .... (F.)
48 Miss B. C. Potter ⑬ ...... (U.S.A.)
49 Miss W. M. Turnbull ⑨ .... (A.)
50 Miss S. A. Walpole .... (G.B.)
51 Miss V. L. Nelson .... (U.S.A.)
52 Miss A. J. Brown .... (U.S.A.)
53 Miss C. Jexell .... (SW.)
54 Miss F. Raschiatore .... (I.)
55 Miss S. Cherneva ...... (U.S.S.R.)
56 Miss L. Romanov .... (RU.)
57 Miss J. A. Salmon .... (G.B.)
58 Miss L. Arraya .... (PE.)
59 Miss B. A. Mould .... (S.A.)
60 Miss K. J. Brasher .... (G.B.)
61 Miss V. Ruzici .... (RU.)
62 Miss R. D. Fairbank .... (S.A.)
63 Miss H. A. Ludloff .... (U.S.A.)
64 Miss K. Jordan ⑥ .... (U.S.A.)
65 Miss E. K. Horvath ⑧ .... (U.S.A.)
66 Miss G. Purdy .... (U.S.A.)
67 Miss B. Bunge .... (MON.)
68 Miss H. Pelletier .... (C.)
69 Miss S. Barker .... (G.B.)
70 Miss B. Mentz .... (S.A.)
71 Miss S. E. Mascarin ...... (U.S.A.)
72 Miss S. Graf .... (G.)
73 Miss K. Rinaldi .... (U.S.A.)
74 Miss K. A. Steinmetz .... (U.S.A.)
75 Mrs. H. A. Mochizuki .... (U.S.A.)
76 Miss S. Skronska .... (CZ.)
77 Miss K. Y. Sands .... (U.S.A.)
78 Miss E. M. Burgin .... (U.S.A.)
79 Mrs. L. A. Shaefer ...... (U.S.A.)
80 Miss J. M. Durie ⑩ .... (G.B.)
81 Miss H. Sukova ⑭ .... (CZ.)
82 Miss R. Reggi .... (IT.)
83 Miss K. B. Cummings .. (U.S.A.)
84 Miss A. M. Cecchini .... (IT.)
85 Miss P. Huber .... (AU.)
86 Miss P. Casale .... (U.S.A.)
87 Miss P. Vasquez .... (PE.)
88 Miss S. L. Acker .... (U.S.A.)
89 Miss K. Kinney .... (U.S.A.)
90 Miss P. A. Teeguarden .. (U.S.A.)
91 Miss C. Tanvier .... (F.)
92 Miss S. E. Reeves .... (G.B.)
93 Miss C. Lindqvist .... (SW.)
94 Miss L. E. Allen .... (U.S.A.)
95 Miss E. Eliseenko ...... (U.S.S.R.)
96 Miss H. Mandlikova ③ ...... (CZ.)
97 Miss Z. L. Garrison ⑤ .... (U.S.A.)
98 Miss R. L. Einy .... (G.B.)
99 Miss A. B. Henricksson .. (U.S.A.)
100 Miss S. V. Wade .... (G.B.)
101 Miss C. Jolissaint .... (SWZ.)
102 Miss L. McNeil .... (U.S.A.)
103 Miss C. Karlsson .... (SW.)
104 Miss A. H. White .... (U.S.A.)
105 Miss S. Amiach .... (F.)
106 Miss L. Antonoplis ...... (U.S.A.)
107 Miss T. A. Holladay ...... (U.S.A.)
108 Miss S. J. Leo .... (A.)
109 Miss C. C. Monteiro .... (BR.)
110 Miss A. M. Fernandez .. (U.S.A.)
111 Miss J. S. Golder .... (U.S.A.)
112 Miss A. Temesvari ⑮ .... (HU.)
113 Miss C. Kohde-Kilsch ⑫ .. (G.)
114 Miss B. C. Bramblett .... (U.S.A.)
115 Miss T. Phelps .... (U.S.A.)
116 Miss S. Simmonds .... (IT.)
117 Miss S. L. Gomer .... (G.B.)
118 Mrs. Kiyomura-Hayashi (U.S.A.)
119 Miss N. S. Yeargin ...... (U.S.A.)
120 Miss A. L. Minter .... (A.)
121 Miss M. Y. Torres .... (U.S.A.)
122 Miss P. S. Medrado .... (BR.)
123 Mrs. P. Delhees-Jauch .. (SWZ.)
124 Miss A. N. Croft .... (G.B.)
125 Miss B. Nagelsen .... (U.S.A.)
126 Miss R. Casals .... (U.S.A.)
127 Miss S. Goles .... (YU.)
128 Mrs. J. M. Lloyd ② ...... (U.S.A.)

SECOND ROUND

Miss M. Navratilova ① 6-4, 6-0
Miss A. E. Holton 6-4, 7-6
Miss A. A. Moulton 6-4, 6-1
Miss I. Budarova 7-6, 6-2
Miss G. A. Rush 4-6, 6-4, 6-1
Miss E. M. Sayers 6-2, 6-3
Miss B. Gerken 6-1, 6-2
Miss L. Bonder ⑪ 2-6, 6-3, 6-3
Miss C. Bassett ⑥ 6-1, 3-6, 6-3
Miss M. C. Calleja 5-7, 6-3, 6-2
Miss M. L. Piatek 6-2, 2-6, 10-8
Miss A. E. Hobbs 6-2, 7-6
Miss J. L. Klitch 6-3, 6-2
Miss Y. Vermaak 7-6, 6-1
Miss N. Reva 6-3, 7-6
Miss M. Maleeva ⑦ 6-4, 6-1
Miss P. H. Shriver ④ 6-0, 6-4
Miss G. Fernandez 7-6, 6-4
Miss W. E. White 7-6, 7-6
Miss C. Benjamin 3-6, 6-4
Miss M. L. Brown 7-5, 1-6, 6-4
Miss M. Skuherska 6-1, 6-2
Miss G. M. Kim 7-6, 1-6, 6-0
Miss B. C. Potter ⑬ 7-5, 6-3
Miss W. M. Turnbull ⑨ 6-3, 6-2
Miss A. J. Brown 6-4, 6-1
Miss F. Raschiatore 6-4, 6-4
Miss S. Cherneva 1-6, 6-4, 6-4
Miss J. A. Salmon 6-4, 6-3
Miss B. A. Mould 6-3, 6-4
Miss V. Ruzici 6-1, 6-4
Miss K. Jordan ⑥ 6-1, 6-1
Miss E. K. Horvath ⑧ 6-4, 6-3
Miss B. Bunge 6-1, 6-2
Miss S. Barker 2-6, 6-4, 6-4
Miss S. Graf 6-4, 5-7, 10-8
Miss K. A. Steinmetz 6-4, 6-2
Mrs. H. A. Mochizuki 7-6, 6-0
Miss E. M. Burgin 7-6, 3-6, 6-2
Miss J. M. Durie ⑩ 6-2, 6-7, 6-0
Miss H. Sukova ⑭ 6-3, 6-4
Miss A. M. Cecchini 4-6, 6-0
Miss P. Casale 6-1, 6-4
Miss P. Vasquez 7-5, 7-6
Miss P. A. Teeguarden 7-6, 7-6
Miss C. Tanvier 6-7, 6-4, 8-6
Miss C. Lindqvist 6-3, 7-6
Miss H. Mandlikova ③ 6-1, 6-0
Miss Z. L. Garrison ⑤ 6-0, 6-0
Miss S. V. Wade 3-6, 6-3, 6-4
Miss C. Jolissaint 7-5, 2-6, 6-3
Miss C. Karlsson 7-5, 2-6, 8-6
Miss S. Amiach 6-3, 6-1
Miss S. J. Leo 2-6, 6-3, 6-4
Miss C. C. Monteiro 4-6, 6-2, 9-7
Miss A. Temesvari ⑮ 6-4, 6-1
Miss C. Kohde-Kilsch ⑫ 6-1, 6-4
Miss S. Simmonds 7-6, 6-4
Mrs. Kiyomura-Hayashi 6-2, 7-6
Miss A. L. Minter 6-1, 6-4
Miss M. Y. Torres 6-2, 6-7, 10-8
Miss A. N. Croft 6-3, 6-0
Miss B. Nagelsen 6-3, 6-1
Mrs. J. M. Lloyd ② 6-1, 6-1

THIRD ROUND

Miss M. Navratilova ① 6-2, 7-5
Miss I. Budarova 6-4, 6-4
Miss E. M. Sayers 6-4, 3-6, 6-2
Miss L. Bonder ⑪ 7-6, 6-2
Miss C. Bassett ⑥ 6-1, 6-4
Miss A. E. Hobbs 6-4, 6-3
Miss Y. Vermaak 6-3, 6-2
Miss M. Maleeva ⑦ 6-2, 6-2
Miss P. H. Shriver ④ 3-6, 6-3, 9-7
Miss C. Benjamin 7-5, 6-3
Miss M. Skuherska 6-4, 6-4
Miss B. C. Potter ⑬ 6-3, 6-0
Miss W. M. Turnbull ⑨ 6-3, 6-4
Miss S. Cherneva 6-3, 6-4
Miss J. A. Salmon 6-4, 7-6
Miss K. Jordan ⑥ 6-4, 6-4
Miss B. Bunge 6-0, 6-4
Miss S. Graf 7-6, 6-3
Miss K. A. Steinmetz 7-6, 6-3
Miss J. M. Durie ⑩ 6-1, 6-3
Miss H. Sukova ⑭ 6-3, 6-0
Miss P. Casale 6-2, 6-0
Miss C. Tanvier 6-1, 6-4
Miss H. Mandlikova ③ 7-5, 6-3
Miss S. V. Wade 3-6, 6-4, 7-5
Miss C. Karlsson 2-6, 6-3, 6-4
Miss S. J. Leo 4-1, ret'd
Miss A. Temesvari ⑮ 6-4, 6-1
Miss C. Kohde-Kilsch ⑫ 6-1, 6-2
Mrs. Kiyomura-Hayashi 6-3, 1-6, 12-10
Miss A. N. Croft 6-3, 2-6, 7-5
Mrs. J. M. Lloyd ② 6-2, 4-6, 6-2

FOURTH ROUND

Miss M. Navratilova ① 6-2, 6-2
Miss E. M. Sayers 6-4, 6-2
Miss A. E. Hobbs 7-6, 3-6, 6-4
Miss M. Maleeva ⑦ 6-4, 6-4
Miss P. H. Shriver ④ 6-0, 6-2
Miss B. C. Potter ⑬ 6-1, 6-3
Miss W. M. Turnbull ⑨ 6-3, 4-6, 6-4
Miss K. Jordan ⑥ 6-4, 6-3
Miss S. Graf 7-5, 6-3
Miss J. M. Durie ⑩ 6-4, 6-2
Miss H. Sukova ⑭ 7-6, 6-7, 6-4
Miss H. Mandlikova ③ 6-4, 7-6
Miss C. Karlsson 6-2, 4-6, 11-9
Miss A. Temesvari ⑮ 6-2, 6-2
Miss C. Kohde-Kilsch ⑫ 6-3, 6-1
Mrs. J. M. Lloyd ② 6-3, 6-4

QUARTER-FINALS

Miss M. Navratilova ① 6-0, ret'd
Miss M. Maleeva ⑦ 6-2, 3-6, 6-3
Miss P. H. Shriver ④ 6-4, 6-3
Miss K. Jordan ⑥ 6-2, 6-3
Miss J. M. Durie ⑩ 3-6, 6-3, 9-7
Miss H. Sukova ⑭ 7-6, 6-7, 6-4
Miss C. Karlsson 6-4, 7-5
Mrs. J. M. Lloyd ② 6-2, 6-4

SEMI-FINALS

Miss M. Navratilova ① 6-3, 6-2
Miss K. Jordan ⑥ 2-6, 6-3, 6-4
Miss H. Mandlikova ③ 6-1, 6-4
Mrs. J. M. Lloyd ② 6-1, 6-2

FINAL

Miss M. Navratilova ① 6-3, 6-4
Mrs. J. M. Lloyd ② 6-2, 6-2

Miss M. Navratilova ① 7-6, 6-2

Heavy type denotes seeded players. The encircled figure against names denotes the order in which they have been seeded.

Event IV.—THE LADIES' DOUBLES CHAMPIONSHIP

The Winners become the holders, for the year, of the CHALLENGE CUP presented by H.R.H. PRINCESS MARINA, DUCHESS OF KENT, the late President of The All England Lawn Tennis and Croquet Club. The Winners receive silver replicas of the Challenge Cup. A Silver Medal is presented to each of the Runners-up and a Bronze Medal to each defeated Semi-finalist.

	FIRST ROUND	SECOND ROUND	THIRD ROUND	QUARTER-FINALS	SEMI-FINALS	FINAL
1	**Miss M. Navratilova and Miss P. H. Shriver** ①	**Miss M. Navratilova and Miss P. H. Shriver** ① 6–1, 6–1	Miss M. Navratilova and Miss P. H. Shriver ① 6–4, 6–1	Miss M. Navratilova and Miss P. H. Shriver ① 6–0, 6–0	Miss M Navratilova and Miss P. H Shriver ① 6–7, 6–4, 6–2	Miss M. Navratilova and Miss P. H. Shriver ① 6–3, 6–4
2	Miss P. Casale and Miss L. Romanov					
3	Miss T. Phelps and Miss M. Y. Torres	Miss M. Louie and Miss H. A. Ludloff 7–6, 7–5				
4	Miss M. Louie and Miss H. A. Ludloff					
5	Miss I. S. Kloss and Miss B. F. Stove	Miss L. Bonder and Miss S. E. Mascarin 6–3, 6–1	Miss L. Bonder and Miss S.E. Mascarin w o			
6	Miss L. Bonder and Miss S. E. Mascarin					
7	Miss K. T. Copeland and Miss J. M. Hetherington	**Miss Z. L. Garrison and Miss L. McNeil** ⑯ 6–4, 7–5				
8	**Miss Z. L. Garrison and Miss L. McNeil** ⑯					
9	**Miss M. Jausovec and Miss S. V. Wade** ⑫	**Miss M. Jausovec and Miss S. V. Wade** ⑫ 7–5, 6–2	Miss M. Jausovec and Miss S.V. Wade ⑫ 6–1, 6–3	Miss C. Kohde-Kilsch and Miss H. Mandlikova ⑧ 6–3, 2–6, 6–0		
10	Miss J. A. Mundel and Miss R. Uys					
11	Miss S. Copeland and Mrs. H. A. Mochizuki	Miss C.J. Newton and Miss P.J. Whytcross 6–3, 6–4				
12	Miss C. J. Newton and Miss P. J. Whytcross					
13	Miss S. L. Acker and Miss B. Nagelsen	Miss S. L. Acker and Miss B. Nagelsen 6–4, 6–7, 6–3	Miss C Kohde-Kilsch and Miss H. Mandlikova ⑧			
14	Miss H. A. Crowe and Miss K. A. Steinmetz					
15	Miss G. Purdy and Miss R. Reggi	**Miss C. Kohde-Kilsch and Miss H. Mandlikova** ⑧ 7–5, 6–0				
16	**Miss C. Kohde-Kilsch and Miss H. Mandlikova** ⑧					
17	**Miss E. K. Horvath and Miss V. Ruzici** ③	Miss S. Cherneva and Miss L. Savchenko 6–4, 6–3	Miss S. Cherneva and Miss L. Savchenko 6–4, 6–3	Miss S. Cherneva and Miss L. Savchenko 3–6, 7–6, 14–12	Miss J. M. Durie and Mrs. Kiyomura-Hayashi ⑥ 1–6, 6–4, 6–4	
18	Miss S. Cherneva and Miss L. Savchenko					
19	Miss B. J. Remilton and Miss N. Sato	Miss L. Antonoplis and Miss B. A. Mould 6–4, 6–2				
20	Miss L. Antonoplis and Miss B. A. Mould					
21	Miss K. B. Cummings and Miss R. M. White	Mrs. J. M. Lloyd and Miss C. Tanvier 6–4, 7–6	Mrs. J. M. Lloyd and Miss C. Tanvier 6–3, 3–6, 6–2			
22	Mrs. J. M. Lloyd and Miss C. Tanvier					
23	Miss M. Quinlan and Miss M. Van Nostrand	**Miss B. K. Jordan and Miss E. M. Sayers** ③ 6–4, 6–2				
24	**Miss B. K. Jordan and Miss E. M. Sayers** ③					
25	**Miss C. Jolissaint and Miss M. A. Mesker** ⑩	Miss C. Jolissaint and Miss M. A. Mesker ⑩ 6–2, 6–4	Miss C. Benjamin and Miss F. Raschiatore 1–6, 6–3, 6–4	Miss J. M. Durie and Mrs. Kiyomura-Hayashi ⑥ 6–2, 6–4		
26	Miss S. P. Foltz and Miss N. F. Gregory					
27	Miss S. L. Gomer and Miss J. A. Salmon	Miss C. Benjamin and Miss F. Raschiatore 6–2, 6–3				
28	Miss C. Benjamin and Miss F. Raschiatore					
29	Miss C. C. Monteiro and Miss Y. Vermaak	Miss C. C. Monteiro and Miss Y. Vermaak 6–1, 6–2	Miss J. M. Durie and Mrs. Kiyomura-Hayashi ⑥ 6–2, 6–4			
30	Miss L. C. Gracie and Miss E. S. Jones					
31	Miss L. Drescher and Miss E. Inoue	**Miss J. M. Durie and Mrs. Kiyomura-Hayashi** ⑥ 6–1, 6–3				
32	**Miss J. M. Durie and Mrs. Kiyomura-Hayashi** ⑥					
33	**Miss R. D. Fairbank and Miss C. S. Reynolds** ⑤	**Miss R. D. Fairbank and Miss C. S. Reynolds** ⑤ 6–1, 6–1	Miss R.D. Fairbank and Miss C.S. Reynolds ⑤ 6–3, 6–2	Miss R.D. Fairbank and Miss C.S. Reynolds ⑤ 6–3, 6–4	Miss B. C. Potter and Miss S. A. Walsh ④ 7–6, 6–4	Miss K. Jordan and Miss A. E. Smith ⑦ 3–6, 6–3, 6–2
34	Miss S. Anderholm and Miss M. Yanagi					
35	Miss K. Y. Sands and Miss C. Vanier	Miss K. Y. Sands and Miss C. Vanier 6–1, 6–2				
36	Miss A. L. Minter and Miss E. A. Minter					
37	Miss A. Jexell and Miss J. L. Klitch	Miss A. B. Henricksson and Miss N. S. Yeargin 7–6, 5–7, 10–8	Miss L.E. Allen and Miss A.H. White ⑪ 6–3, 3–6, 6–3			
38	Miss A. B. Henricksson and Miss N. S. Yeargin					
39	Miss I. Budarova and Miss M. Skuherska	**Miss L. E. Allen and Miss A. H. White** ⑪ 6–0, 7–5				
40	**Miss L. E. Allen and Miss A. H. White** ⑪					
41	Miss K. Kinney and Miss R. Mentz	Miss K. Kinney and Miss R. Mentz 6–3, 6–1	Miss G. Fernandez and Miss A. A. Moulton 6–0, 6–2	Miss B. C. Potter and Miss S. A. Walsh ④ 6–3, 6–4		
42	Miss H. Manset and Miss S. A. Margolin					
43	Miss A. J. Brown and Miss A. M. Fernandez	Miss G. Fernandez and Miss A. A. Moulton 6–2, 6–2				
44	Miss G. Fernandez and Miss A. A. Moulton					
45	Miss P. Barg and Miss A. E. Holton	Miss C. Bassett and Miss A. Temesvari 6–3, 6–2	Miss B. C. Potter and Miss S. A. Walsh ④ 6–3, 6–4			
46	Miss C. Bassett and Miss A. Temesvari					
47	Miss S. Goles and Miss P. Huber	**Miss B. C. Potter and Miss S. A. Walsh** ④ 6–2, 6–1				
48	**Miss B. C. Potter and Miss S. A. Walsh** ④					
49	**Miss K. Jordan and Miss A. E. Smith** ⑦	Miss K. Jordan and Miss A. E. Smith ⑦ 7–5, 6–3	Miss K. Jordan and Miss A. E. Smith ⑦ 6–0, 6–2	Miss K. Jordan and Miss A. E. Smith ⑦ 6–2, 6–0	Miss K. Jordan and Miss A. E. Smith ⑦ 6–0, 6–1	
50	Miss M. Maleeva and Miss H. Sukova					
51	Miss T. A. Holladay and Mrs. L. A. Shaefer	Miss A. M. Cecchini and Miss S. Simmonds 6–4, 6–7, 6–2				
52	Miss A. M. Cecchini and Miss S. Simmonds					
53	Miss S. Graf and Miss B. Norton	Miss E. Eliseenko and Miss N. Reva 4–6, 6–1, 8–6	Miss P.G. Smith and Miss W.E. White 6–2, 7–5			
54	Miss E. Eliseenko and Miss N. Reva					
55	Miss P. G. Smith and Miss W. E. White	Miss P. G. Smith and Miss W. E. White 7–6, 7–5				
56	**Miss B. Bunge and Miss E. S. Pfaff** ⑭					
57	**Miss A. C. Leand and Miss M. L. Piatek** ⑨	Miss A. C. Leand and Miss M. L. Piatek ⑨ 6–7, 6–3, 6–4	Miss R. L. Blount and Mrs. F. I. Wright 6–0, 7–6	Miss R.L. Blount and Mrs. F.I. Wright 6–3, 3–6, 9–7		
58	Miss N. Herreman and Miss C. Suire					
59	Miss R. L. Blount and Miss F. I. Wright	Miss R. L. Blount and Mrs. F. I. Wright 7–6, 6–1				
60	Miss I. Kuczynska and Miss S. J. Leo					
61	Miss R. L. Einy and Miss K. Rimes	Miss S. L. Collins and Miss P. S. Medrado 6–1, 6–0	Miss S. L. Collins and Miss P. S. Medrado 7–6, 6–4			
62	Miss S. L. Collins and Miss P. S. Medrado					
63	Miss B. Herr and Miss P. A. Teeguarden	**Miss A. E. Hobbs and Miss W. M. Turnbull** ⑮ 6–2, 6–2				
64	**Miss A. E. Hobbs and Miss W. M. Turnbull** ⑮					

Heavy type denotes seeded players. The encircled figure against names denotes the order in which they have been seeded.

154

Event V.—THE MIXED DOUBLES CHAMPIONSHIP

The Winners become the holders, for the year, of the CHALLENGE CUP presented by the family of the late Mr. S. H. SMITH. The Winners receive silver replicas of the Challenge Cup. A Silver Medal is presented to each of the Runners-up and a Bronze Medal to each defeated Semi-finalist.

FIRST ROUND	SECOND ROUND	THIRD ROUND	QUARTER-FINALS	SEMI-FINALS	FINAL
1 J. M. Lloyd and Miss W. M. Turnbull ①	J. M. Lloyd and Miss W. M. Turnbull ① 6–4, 6–4	J. M. Lloyd and Miss W. M. Turnbull ① 6–3, 6–4	J. M. Lloyd and Miss W. M. Turnbull ① 6–2, 6–2	J. M. Lloyd and Miss W. M. Turnbull ① 6–3, 3–6, 6–2	J. M. Lloyd and Miss W.M. Turnbull ① 6–3, 6–3
2 J. D. Newcombe and Miss A. C. Leand					
3 M. T. Fancutt and Miss C. S. Reynolds	M. T. Fancutt and Miss C. S. Reynolds w o				
4 B. Testerman and Miss R. Casals		A. Amritraj and Miss S. L. Acker 4–6, 7–6, 6–2			
5 G. Whitecross and Miss J. M. Hetherington	G. Whitecross and Miss J. M. Hetherington 7–5, 6–2				
6 B. Walts and Miss S. E. Mascarin					
7 A. Amritraj and Miss S. L. Acker	A. Amritraj and Miss S. L. Acker 6–3, 3–6, 6–3				
8 B. Dyke and Miss H. Strachonova					
9 O. K. Davidson and Miss I. S. Kloss	M. Depalmer and Miss S. Goles 4–6, 6–3, 7–5	L. Warder and Miss A. L. Minter 6–4, 7–6	L. Warder and Miss A. L. Minter 7–5, 7–6		
10 M. Depalmer and Miss S. Goles					
11 R. J. Simpson and Miss B. M. Perry	L. Warder and Miss A. L. Minter 4–6, 6–2, 6–2				
12 L. Warder and Miss A. L. Minter					
13 M. W. C. Guntrip and Miss H. A. Ludloff	M. Purcell and Miss P. G. Smith 4–6, 7–6, 6–4	M. Purcell and Miss P. G. Smith 6–3, 6–1			
14 M. Purcell and Miss P. G. Smith					
15 D. Graham and Miss B. Herr	R. R. Grant and Miss A. L. Gulley 6–4, 6–1				
16 R. R. Grant and Miss A. L. Gulley					
17 M. Estep and Miss M. Navratilova ④	M. Estep and Miss M. Navratilova ④ 6–1, 6–2	M. Estep and Miss M. Navratilova ④ 6–3, 6–3	M. Estep and Miss M. Navratilova ④ 3–6, 7–5, 6–3	S. E. Stewart and Miss E. M. Sayers ⑦ 6–1, 6–4	
18 K. Flach and Miss F. Raschiatore					
19 J. W. Feaver and Miss S. V. Wade	J. W. Feaver and Miss S. V. Wade 6–4, 6–4				
20 M. Davis and Miss M. L. Piatek					
21 S. Ball and Mrs. L. A. Shaefer	B. M. Mitton and Miss P. A. Teeguarden 6–4, 6–4	G. Holmes and Miss C. Bassett 6–4, 1–0 ret'd			
22 B. M. Mitton and Miss P. A. Teeguarden					
23 B. H. Levine and Miss Y. Vermaak	G. Holmes and Miss C. Bassett 6–1, 6–2				
24 G. Holmes and Miss C. Bassett					
25 C. Dowdeswell and Miss E. Inoue	C. Dowdeswell and Miss E. Inoue 7–6, 6–4	C. Dowdeswell and Miss E. Inoue 5–7, 6–1, 6–3	S. E. Stewart and Miss E. M. Sayers ⑦ 4–6, 6–4, 6–2		
26 R. C. Lutz and Miss L. E. Allen					
27 D. A. Lloyd and Miss S. Barker	D. A. Lloyd and Miss S. Barker 6–3, 7–6				
28 R. A. Lewis and Miss M. Y. Torres					
29 C. M. Johnstone and Miss P. J. Whytcross	C. Motta and Miss C. C. Monteiro 6–2, 7–5	S. E. Stewart and Miss E. M. Sayers ⑦ 6–3, 3–6, 6–0			
30 C. Motta and Miss C. C. Monteiro					
31 M. N. Doyle and Miss K. Y. Sands	S. E. Stewart and Miss E. M. Sayers ⑦ w o				
32 S. E. Stewart and Miss E. M. Sayers ⑦					
33 M. C. Riessen and Miss A. E. Hobbs ⑧	M. C. Riessen and Miss A. E. Hobbs ⑧ 6–3, 4–6, 6–3	M. C. Riessen and Miss A. E. Hobbs ⑧ 6–3, 6–2	M. C. Riessen and Miss A. E. Hobbs ⑧ 6–3, 6–2	A. Giammalva and Miss S. A. Walsh 3–6, 6–2, 10–8	
34 M. Kratzmann and Miss J. Byrne					
35 C. S. Dibley and Mrs. D. E. Dalton	S. M. Bale and Miss R. L. Einy 7–6, 7–6				
36 S. M. Bale and Miss R. L. Einy					
37 C. M. Dunk and Miss B. K. Jordan	D. Gitlin and Miss M. A. Mesker 7–6, 7–5	P. Doohan and Miss N. A. Leipus 6–4, 7–5			
38 D. Gitlin and Miss M. A. Mesker					
39 P. Doohan and Miss N. A. Leipus	P. Doohan and Miss N. A. Leipus 6–4, 7–5				
40 J. M. Dier and Miss J. A. Mundel					
41 M. Mortensen and Miss T. Scheuer-Larsen	A. Giammalva and Miss S. A. Walsh 4–6, 6–4, 6–4	A. Giammalva and Miss S. A. Walsh 7–5, 7–5	A. Giammalva and Miss S. A. Walsh 6–2, 6–1		
42 A. Giammalva and Miss S. A. Walsh					
43 V. C. Amaya and Miss A. N. Croft	P. Rennert and Miss C. Tanvier 6–2, 6–3				
44 P. Rennert and Miss C. Tanvier					
45 R. Seguso and Miss J. S. Golder	R. Seguso and Miss J. S. Golder 5–7, 7–6, 6–3	R. L. Stockton and Miss A. E. Smith ③ 6–3, 6–2			
46 F. D. McMillan and Miss B. F. Stove					
47 S. Meister and Miss P. Barg	R. L. Stockton and Miss A. E. Smith ③ w o				
48 R. L. Stockton and Miss A. E. Smith ③					
49 K. Curren and Miss A. Temesvari ⑤	K. Curren and Miss A. Temesvari ⑤ 6–0, 6–2	K. Curren and Miss A. Temesvari ⑤ 7–6, 6–0	K. Curren and Miss A. Temesvari ⑤ 6–1, 7–6	S. Denton and Miss K. Jordan ② 7–5, 7–5	
50 R. J. Moore and Miss R. Mentz					
51 C. Van Rensburg and Miss B. A. Mould	C. Bradnam and Miss A. J. Brown 2–6, 6–3, 7–5				
52 C. Bradnam and Miss A. J. Brown					
53 C. D. Strode and Miss R. D. Fairbank	C. D. Strode and Miss R. D. Fairbank 7–5, 6–7, 6–3	C. D. Strode and Miss R. D. Fairbank 7–6, 6–4			
54 C. A. Miller and Miss B. J. Remilton					
55 G. Barbosa and Miss P. S. Medrado	G. Barbosa and Miss P. S. Medrado w o				
56 R. Harmon and Miss Z. L. Garrison					
57 T. E. Gullikson and Miss S. Simmonds	J. Fillol and Miss P. Casale 7–5, 4–6, 6–3	J. Fillol and Miss P. Casale 7–5, 6–4	S. Denton and Miss K. Jordan ② 6–3, 6–7, 6–1		
58 J. Fillol and Miss P. Casale					
59 L. Stefanki and Miss A. H. White	L. Stefanki and Miss A. H. White 6–2, 7–6				
60 J. B. Fitzgerald and Miss B. Nagelsen					
61 C. H. Cox and Miss W. E. White	C. H. Cox and Miss W. E. White 6–3, 4–6, 8–6	S. Denton and Miss K. Jordan ② 7–5, 6–2			
62 R. D. Ralston and Miss C. Benjamin					
63 L. R. Bourne and Miss A. A. Moulton	S. Denton and Miss K. Jordan ② 6–2, 6–7, 6–4				
64 S. Denton and Miss K. Jordan ②					

J. M. Lloyd and Miss W.M. Turnbull ① 6–3, 6–3

Heavy type denotes seeded players. The encircled figure against names denotes the order in which they have been seeded.

Event VI.—THE ALL ENGLAND LADIES' PLATE

Players who are beaten in the first or second round of the Ladies' Singles Championship and also players only taking part in the Doubles events are entitled to enter for this Event. The Winner becomes the holder, for the year only, of a Silver Cup "The All England Ladies' Plate", presented to The All England Lawn Tennis and Croquet Club by the late Mr. A. H. RISELEY, O.B.E. The Winner receives a silver miniature of the Trophy.

FIRST ROUND

1. Miss A. Leand ① ...... (U.S.A.)
2. Bye
3. Miss S. E. Reeves ...... (G.B.)
4. Miss R. L. Blount ...... (U.S.A.)
5. Miss P. J. Whytcross ...... (A.)
6. Miss C. Copeland ...... (U.S.A.)
7. Bye
8. Miss L. Antonoplis ① ...... (U.S.A.)
9. Miss S. A. Walpole ...... (G.B.)
10. Miss K. J. Brasher ...... (G.B.)
11. Miss N. A. Leipus ...... (A.)
12. Bye
13. Miss K. Kinney ...... (U.S.A.)
14. Bye
15. Bye
16. Miss N. Reva ⑦ ...... (U.S.S.R.)
17. Miss M. Louie ④ ...... (U.S.A.)
18. Bye
19. Miss H. Manset ...... (U.S.A.)
20. Miss N. F. Gregory ...... (A.)
21. Bye
22. Miss E. S. Jones ...... (G.B.)
23. Bye
24. Miss B. Gerken ⑨ ...... (U.S.A.)
25. Bye
26. Miss R. M. White ...... (U.S.A.)
27. Miss C. S. Reynolds ...... (U.S.A.)
28. Bye
29. Miss L. C. Gracie ...... (G.B.)
30. Miss B. K. Jordan ...... (U.S.A.)
31. Bye
32. Miss P. S. Medrado ⑤ ...... (BR.)
33. Miss J. S. Golder ⑥ ...... (U.S.A.)
34. Bye
35. Bye
36. Miss H. Pelletier ...... (C.)
37. Miss J. M. Hetherington ...... (C.)
38. Miss S. A. Margolin ......
39. Bye
40. Miss B. M. Perry ...... (N.Z.)
41. Miss A. M. Fernandez ⑩ ...... (U.S.A.)
42. Bye
43. Miss A. L. Gulley ...... (A.)
44. Miss E. A. Minter ...... (A.)
45. Bye
46. Miss S. L. Gomer ...... (G.B.)
47. Bye
48. Miss T. A. Holladay ③ ...... (U.S.A.)
49. Mrs. H. A. Mochizuki ⑧ ...... (U.S.A.)
50. Bye
51. Bye
52. Miss E. Eliseenko ...... (U.S.S.R.)
53. Bye
54. Miss H. A. Crowe ...... (U.S.A.)
55. Bye
56. Miss R. Mentz ⑫ ...... (S.A.)
57. Bye
58. Miss C. J. Newton ...... (N.Z.)
59. Miss S. T. Mair ...... (G.B.)
60. Miss M. Quinlan ...... (U.S.A.)
61. Miss J. Louis ...... (G.B.)
62. Miss K. T. Copeland ...... (U.S.A.)
63. Bye
64. Miss M. L. Brown ② ...... (U.S.A.)

SECOND ROUND

- Miss A. Leand ①
- Miss S. E. Reeves — 6-4, 6-3
- Miss P. J. Whytcross — 1-6, 6-4, 7-5
- Miss L. Antonoplis ①
- Miss K. J. Brasher — 6-3, 7-6
- Miss N. A. Leipus
- Miss K. Kinney
- Miss N. Reva ⑦
- Miss M. Louie ④
- Miss N. F. Gregory — 6-3, 6-1
- Miss E. S. Jones
- Miss B. Gerken ⑨
- Miss R. M. White
- Miss C. S. Reynolds
- Miss B. K. Jordan — 6-4, 3-6, 9-7
- Miss P. S. Medrado ⑤
- Miss J. S. Golder ⑥
- Miss H. Pelletier
- Miss J. M. Hetherington — 6-2, 6-2
- Miss B. M. Perry
- Miss A. M. Fernandez ⑩
- Miss E. A. Minter — 6-4, 6-2
- Miss S. L. Gomer
- Miss T. A. Holladay ③
- Mrs. H. A. Mochizuki ⑧
- Miss E. Eliseenko
- Miss H. A. Crowe
- Miss R. Mentz ⑫
- Miss C. J. Newton
- Miss S. T. Mair — 6-3, 2-6, 6-2
- Miss J. Louis — 6-4, 7-5
- Miss M. L. Brown ②

THIRD ROUND

- Miss S. E. Reeves — 6-4, 6-2
- Miss L. Antonoplis ① — 6-2, 6-4
- Miss N. A. Leipus — 6-2, 6-3
- Miss N. Reva ⑦ — 6-4, 6-4
- Miss M. Louie ④ — 6-4, 1-6, 6-4
- Miss B. Gerken ⑨ — 4-6, 7-6, 6-2
- Miss R. M. White — w o
- Miss B. K. Jordan — 6-4, 6-3
- Miss J. S. Golder ⑥ — 6-2, 3-6, 7-5
- Miss J.M. Hetherington — 6-2, 3-6, 7-5
- Miss A.M. Fernandez ⑩ — 5-7, 7-5, 6-3
- Miss T. A. Holladay ③ — 6-4, 2-6, 6-2
- Miss E. Eliseenko — 7-6, 6-4
- Miss H. A. Crowe — 4-6, 6-4, 6-4
- Miss S. T. Mair — 6-1, 6-3
- Miss M. L. Brown ② — 6-3, 7-6

QUARTER-FINALS

- Miss L. Antonoplis ① — 6-1, 7-5
- Miss N. Reva ⑦ — 7-6, 6-1
- Miss B. Gerken ⑨ — 6-1, 7-5
- Miss R. M. White — 6-3, 6-4
- Miss J. S. Golder ⑥ — 4-6, 6-1, 9-7
- Miss T.A. Holladay ③ — 6-1, 1-6, 6-3
- Miss E. Eliseenko — 7-5, 6-4
- Miss M. L. Brown ② — 6-4, 6-4

SEMI-FINALS

- Miss L. Antonoplis ① — 6-3, 5-7, 6-2
- Miss R. M. White — 6-0, 6-1
- Miss J. S. Golder ⑥ — 1-6, 7-5, 4-0, Ret'd.
- Miss M. L. Brown ② — 3-6, 6-2, 6-1

FINAL

- Miss R. M. White — 6-4, 6-1
- Miss M. L. Brown ② — 4-6, 6-4

WINNER: Miss M. L. Brown ② — 6-2, 7-5

The Matches will be the best of three sets.

Event VII.—THE 35 AND OVER GENTLEMEN'S INVITATION SINGLES

The Winner becomes the holder, for the year only, of a Cup presented by The All England Lawn Tennis and Croquet Club. The Winner receives a miniature Silver Salver, the Runner-up is presented with a Silver Medal.

FIRST ROUND	QUARTER-FINALS	SEMI-FINALS	FINAL	
1 S. R. Smith ① .... (U.S.A.) 2 T. S. Okker .... (NTH.)	S. R. Smith ① 6–3, 7–5	S. R. Smith ① 7–6, 7–6	S. R. Smith ① 4–6, 7–5, 6–3	S. R. Smith ① 7–6, 6–3
3 M. Cox .... (G.B.) 4 F. S. Stolle .... (A.)	M. Cox 7–6, 6–4			
5 J. Fillol ③ .... (CH.) 6 R. A. J. Hewitt .... (S.A.)	J. Fillol ③ 6–2, 6–4	J. Fillol ③ 6–3, 6–4		
7 R. Taylor .... (G.B.) 8 R. C. Lutz .... (U.S.A.)	R. C. Lutz 4–6, 6–3, 7–5			
9 J. D. Newcombe .... (A.) 10 M. C. Riessen .... (U.S.A.)	M. C. Riessen 6–1, 6–4	M. C. Riessen 6–4, 6–2	C. S. Dibley ② 7–6, 6–3	
11 F. D. McMillan .... (S.A.) 12 K. R. Rosewall ④ .... (A.)	K. R. Rosewall ④ 6–1, 6–2			
13 S. E. Stewart .... (U.S.A.) 14 O. K. Davidson .... (A.)	S. E. Stewart 6–3, 7–6	C. S. Dibley ② 6–3, 6–7, 6–4		
15 R. J. Moore .... (S.A.) 16 C. S. Dibley ② .... (A.)	C. S. Dibley ② 6–4, 6–1			

Event VIII.—THE 35 AND OVER GENTLEMEN'S INVITATION DOUBLES

The Winners become the holders, for the year only, of a Cup presented by The All England Lawn Tennis and Croquet Club. The Winners receive miniature Silver Salvers, a Silver Medal is presented to each of the Runners-up.

FIRST ROUND	SEMI-FINALS	FINAL	
1 R. C. Lutz and C. M. Pasarell ① 2 M. Cox and T. S. Okker	M. Cox and T. S. Okker 6–4, 2–6, 6–4	C. S. Dibley and J. Fillol 6–3, 7–5	M. C. Riessen and S. E. Stewart ② 6–3, 3–6, 10–8
3 O. K. Davidson and J. D. Newcombe ④ 4 C. S. Dibley and J. Fillol	C. S. Dibley and J. Fillol 6–4, 1–6, 15–13		
5 R. J. Moore and R. Taylor 6 K. R. Rosewall and F. S. Stolle ③	K. R. Rosewall and F. S. Stolle ③ 7–6, 6–2	M. C. Riessen and S. E. Stewart ② 6–2, 7–5	
7 R. A. J. Hewitt and F. D. McMillan 8 M. C. Riessen and S. E. Stewart ②	M. C. Riessen and S. E. Stewart ② 4–6, 6–4, 6–4		

EVENT IX.—THE BOYS' SINGLES CHAMPIONSHIP

The Winner becomes the holder, for the year only, of a Cup presented by The All England Lawn Tennis and Croquet Club. The Winner and Runner-up each receive a personal prize.

FIRST ROUND

1. S. Botfield (G.B.)
2. S. Kruger (S.A.)
3. H. Aslem (PAK.)
4. R. Simon (NTH.)
5. H. J. Choi (KOR.)
6. L. Lavalle (M.)
7. F. Garcia-Lleo (SP.)
8. D. MacPherson [14] (A.)
9. L. Jensen [9] (U.S.A.)
10. M. Gurr (ZIM.)
11. G. Bloom (ISR.)
12. E. Polo (K.)
13. H. Aiyar (IN.)
14. P. A. Coyle (G.B.)
15. M. Rodriguez (CH.)
16. M. Masencamp [8] (S.A.)
17. B. Pearce [4] (U.S.A.)
18. D. Langaskens (B.)
19. G. Ganancia (MON.)
20. C. Suk (CZ.)
21. R. A. W. Whichello (G.B.)
22. C. Grant (H.K.)
23. S. H. Choi (KOR.)
24. A. Antonitsch [16] (AU.)
25. E. Winogradsky [12] (F.)
26. F. Ricci (IT.)
27. M. Nastase (RU.)
28. A. J. W. Brice (G.B.)
29. A. Rezic (V.)
30. S. Ohta (J.)
31. A. Olkhovsky (U.S.S.R.)
32. P. McEnroe [6] (U.S.A.)
33. D. Nahirney [5] (U.S.A.)
34. B. J. Knapp (G.B.)
35. R. Brown (U.S.A.)
36. M. T. Walker (G.B.)
37. M. A. Long (N.Z.)
38. N. Devide (IT.)
39. F. Errard (F.)
40. R. Weiss [15] (U.S.A.)
41. A. Chesnokov [10] (U.S.S.R.)
42. V. Boccitto (V.)
43. M. Tolentino (PH.)
44. S. C. Castello (SP.)
45. S. Bienz (SWZ.)
46. J. A. Daher (BR.)
47. A. Sznajder (C.)
48. J. Svensson [3] (SW.)
49. T. Muster [7] (AU.)
50. J. M. Goodall (G.B.)
51. T. Srichapan (THAI.)
52. C. Allgaardh (SW.)
53. W. Kowalski (POL.)
54. S. C. S. Cole (G.B.)
55. A. Del Rosario (PH.)
56. F. Barrientos [11] (PH.)
57. B. Custer [13] (A.)
58. K. U. Steeb (G.)
59. M. E. Nugent (IRE.)
60. D. Johnson (S.A.)
61. P. Kuehnen (G.)
62. A. Malik (MAL.)
63. M. Tauson (D.)
64. M. Kratzmann [2] (A.)

SECOND ROUND

- S. Kruger 6–1, 6–2
- R. Simon 6–4, 7–5
- L. Lavalle 6–3, 6–2
- F. Garcia-Lleo 7–6, 6–1
- L. Jensen [9] 6–3, 6–0
- G. Bloom 6–1, 6–0
- P. A. Coyle 6–4, 6–1
- M. Rodriguez 2–6, 6–4, 6–4
- B. Pearce [4] 6–3, 6–3
- G. Ganancia 3–6, 7–6, 6–2
- R. A. W. Whichello 6–1, 6–3
- A. Antonitsch [16] 6–2, 6–4
- E. Winogradsky [12] 6–2, 6–4
- M. Nastase 6–2, 6–3
- S. Ohta 6–4, 5–7, 6–0
- P. McEnroe [6] 6–3, 3–6, 6–1
- D. Nahirney [5] 4–6, 7–5, 6–3
- M. T. Walker 7–6, 6–2
- M. A. Long 6–3, 2–6, 7–5
- F. Errard 6–3, 6–4
- A. Chesnokov [10] 6–3, 6–3
- S. C. Castello 7–5, 6–1
- S. Bienz 6–3, 6–1
- J. Svensson [3] 6–2, 6–2
- T. Muster [7] 7–6, 6–3
- C. Allgaardh 6–1, 6–1
- S. C. S. Cole 6–4, 3–6, 6–3
- F. Barrientos [11] 6–3, 5–7, 6–1
- B. Custer [13] 6–4, 6–1
- D. Johnson 6–1, 6–3
- P. Kuehnen 3–6, 7–6, 6–4
- M. Kratzmann [2] 6–3, 3–6, 6–3

THIRD ROUND

- S. Kruger 6–2, 7–6
- F. Garcia-Lleo 4–6, 6–0, 6–2
- L. Jensen [9] 6–2, 6–3
- M. Rodriguez 6–3, 6–2
- B. Pearce [4] 6–0, 6–3
- R. A. W. Whichello 6–1, 5–7, 6–2
- E. Winogradsky [12] 6–3, 6–2
- P. McEnroe [6] 6–3, 7–5
- M. T. Walker 7–5, 6–3
- F. Errard 6–1, 6–1
- A. Chesnokov [10] 6–1, 7–6
- J. Svensson [3] 7–6, 6–1
- C. Allgaardh 5–7, 6–1, 8–6
- F. Barrientos [11] 6–3, 6–0
- B. Custer [13] 6–4, 7–6
- M. Kratzmann [2] 6–4, 6–1

QUARTER-FINALS

- S. Kruger 6–3, 2–6, 6–4
- L. Jensen [9] 7–6, 4–6, 6–4
- B. Pearce [4] 6–7, 7–6, 6–3
- E. Winogradsky [12] 7–6, 6–2
- F. Errard 6–2, 6–4
- J. Svensson [3] 2–6, 6–1, 6–2
- F. Barrientos [11] 6–4, 3–6, 6–3
- M. Kratzmann [2] 6–3, 6–3

(next round)

- S. Kruger 7–6, 6–4
- B. Pearce [4] 6–4, 6–1
- J. Svensson [3] 6–2, 7–5
- M. Kratzmann [2] 6–3, 6–2

SEMI-FINALS

- S. Kruger 7–5, 7–6
- M. Kratzmann [2] 6–4, 6–4

FINAL

- M. Kratzmann [2] 6–4, 4–6, 6–3

EVENT X.—THE BOYS' DOUBLES CHAMPIONSHIP

The Winners and Runners-up each receive a personal prize.

FIRST ROUND

1. M. Kratzmann and J. Svensson [1]
2. B. J. Knapp and R. A. W. Whichello
3. F. Barrientos and A. Del Rosario
4. V. Boccitto and C. Suk
5. D. Nahirney and B. Pearce [4]
6. D. Johnson and M. Masencamp
7. N. Devide and F. Ricci
8. W. Kowalski and D. Langaskens
9. J. M. Goodall and M. T. Walker
10. C. Grant and S. Kruger
11. R. Brown and R. Weiss
12. F. Errard and E. Winogradsky [3]
13. P. Kuehnen and K. U. Steeb
14. S. Bienz and A. Sznajder
15. G. Bloom and M. Nastase
16. L. Jensen and P. McEnroe [2]

SECOND ROUND

- M. Kratzmann and J. Svensson [1] 6–1, 6–4
- V. Boccitto and C. Suk 4–6, 6–0, 7–5
- D. Nahirney and B. Pearce [4] 6–2, 7–6
- N. Devide and F. Ricci 6–3, 6–4
- C. Grant and S. Kruger 4–6, 7–5, 6–4
- R. Brown and R. Weiss 6–4, 7–6
- P. Kuehnen and K. U. Steeb 5–7, 6–3, 7–5
- L. Jensen and P. McEnroe [2] 4–6, 6–3, 6–2

(next round)

- M. Kratzmann and J. Svensson [1] 6–4, 6–3
- D. Nahirney and B. Pearce [4] 6–2, 6–2
- R. Brown and R. Weiss 6–4, 6–4
- P. Kuehnen and K. U. Steeb 6–3, 6–4

SEMI-FINALS

- M. Kratzmann and J. Svensson [1] 4–6, 7–5, 6–4
- R. Brown and R. Weiss 3–6, 6–3, 6–4

FINAL

- R. Brown and R. Weiss 1–6, 6–4, 11–9

EVENT XI.—THE GIRLS' SINGLES CHAMPIONSHIP

The Winner becomes the holder, for the year only, of a Cup presented by The All England Lawn Tennis and Croquet Club. The Winner and Runner-up each receive a personal prize.

	FIRST ROUND	SECOND ROUND	THIRD ROUND	QUARTER-FINALS	SEMI-FINALS	FINAL
1	Miss M. L. Brown ① (U.S.A.)	Miss M. L. Brown ①	Miss M. L. Brown ① 6–4, 6–1			
2	Bye (M.)					
3	Miss C. Hernandez (M.)	Miss C. Hernandez				
4	Bye			Miss S. Rehe 6–3, 6–1		
5	Miss C. Espinoza (CH.)	Miss S. T. Mair 6–2, 6–4				
6	Miss S. T. Mair (G.B.)		Miss S. Rehe 6–0, 6–4			
7	Miss S. Rehe (U.S.A.)	Miss S. Rehe 6–0, 6–1				
8	Miss S. U. Nicholson (IRE.)					
9	Miss K. Schuurmans (B.)	Miss K. Schuurmans 6–4, 7–5			Miss J. Thompson 6–4, 6–1	
10	Miss I. Demongeot (F.)		Miss K. Schuurmans 6–4, 6–4			
11	Bye					
12	Miss E. Iida (J.)	Miss E. Iida		Miss J. Thompson 6–1, 3–6, 6–3		
13	Miss J. Thompson (A.)	Miss J. Thompson 6–1, 7–6	Miss J. Thompson 6–4, 7–5			
14	Miss L. Corsato (BR.)					
15	Bye					
16	Miss S. Campos ⑧ (BR.)	Miss S. Campos ⑧				
17	Miss A. N. Croft ③ (G.B.)	Miss A. N. Croft ③	Miss A. N. Croft ③ 6–1, 6–0			Miss A. N. Croft ③ 4–6, 7–5, 6–1
18	Bye					
19	Miss I. Cueto (G.)	Miss M. Lundquist 6–3, 6–2		Miss A. N. Croft ③ 6–3, 6–0		
20	Miss M. Lundquist (SW.)					
21	Miss J. Louis (G.B.)	Miss J. Louis	Miss J. Louis 7–5, 2–6, 6–1			
22	Bye					
23	Miss K. Maleeva (BUL.)	Miss K. Maleeva 6–4, 6–1			Miss A. N. Croft ③ 6–1, 6–0	
24	Miss P. Moreno (H.K.)					
25	Miss S. P. Foltz (U.S.A.)	Miss S. P. Foltz 6–2, 6–0	Miss S. P. Foltz 6–1, 6–3			
26	Miss J. M. Lee (KOR.)			Miss S. P. Foltz 6–2, 7–6		
27	Bye					
28	Miss J. Novotna (CZ.)	Miss J. Novotna				
29	Miss M. Werdel (U.S.A.)	Miss M. Werdel 6–0, 6–1	Miss M. Paz ⑦ 6–3, 6–4			
30	Miss H. Kelesi (C.)					
31	Bye					
32	Miss M. Paz ⑦ (ARG.)	Miss M. Paz ⑦				
33	Miss L. Savchenko ⑤ (U.S.S.R.)	Miss L. Savchenko ⑤	Miss A. Betzner 7–6, 7–6			
34	Bye					
35	Miss A. Kijimuta (J.)	Miss A. Betzner 6–1, 6–3		Miss E. Reinach 7–5, 6–4		
36	Miss A. Betzner (G.)					
37	Miss A. Grant (G.B.)	Miss A. Grant	Miss E. Reinach 6–2, 6–1			
38	Bye					
39	Miss C. Kuhlman (U.S.A.)	Miss E. Reinach 3–6, 7–6, 6–3			Miss E. Reinach 6–1, 0–6, 7–5	
40	Miss E. Reinach (S.A.)					
41	Miss D. Ketelaar (NTH.)	Miss D. Ketelaar 6–3, 6–0	Miss D. Ketelaar 6–4, 6–2			
42	Miss A. Grunfeld (G.B.)			Miss R. Mentz ④ 6–0, 6–2		Miss E. Reinach 6–2, 4–6, 6–3
43	Miss L. Garrone (IT.)	Miss L. Garrone				
44	Bye					
45	Miss J. Richardson (N.Z.)	Miss M. Yokota 6–4, 6–3	Miss R. Mentz ④ 6–4, 6–2			
46	Miss M. Yokota (J.)					
47	Bye					
48	Miss R. Mentz ④ (S.A.)	Miss R. Mentz ④				
49	Miss N. Diaz ⑥ (BR.)	Miss N. Diaz ⑥	Miss N. Diaz ⑥ w o			
50	Bye					
51	Miss D. Spence (U.S.A.)	Miss D. Spence 6–3, 6–2		Miss N. Diaz ⑥ 6–2, 6–2		
52	Miss N. Rodriguez (CH.)					
53	Miss V. Milvidskaya (U.S.S.R.)	Miss V. Milvidskaya 6–4, 6–4	Miss M. Reinach 3–6, 6–3, 6–4			
54	Miss B. A. Borneo (G.B.)					
55	Bye				Miss E. Krapl 6–4, 6–3	
56	Miss M. Reinach (S.A.)	Miss M. Reinach				
57	Miss S. Schilder (NTH.)	Miss E. Krapl 6–4, 6–4	Miss E. Krapl 6–3, 6–2			
58	Miss E. Krapl (SWZ.)			Miss E. Krapl 5–7, 6–4, 10–8		
59	Miss J. Saberon (PH.)	Miss J. Saberon				
60	Bye					
61	Miss N. Tauziat (F.)	Miss N. Tauziat 6–1, 6–4	Miss M. Torres ② 6–4, 7–6			
62	Miss C. Anderholm (SW.)					
63	Bye					
64	Miss M. Torres ② (COL.)	Miss M. Torres ②				

Winner: Miss A. N. Croft ③ 3–6, 6–3, 6–2

EVENT XII.—THE GIRLS' DOUBLES CHAMPIONSHIP

The Winners and Runners-up each receive a personal prize.

	FIRST ROUND	SECOND ROUND	SEMI-FINALS	FINAL
1	Miss V. Milvidskaya and Miss L. Savchenko ①	Miss V. Milvidskaya and Miss L. Savchenko ① 6–3, 6–0		
2	Miss D. Spence and Miss M. Werdel		Miss V. Milvidskaya and Miss L. Savchenko ① 6–3, 6–4	
3	Miss H. Kelesi and Miss J. Novotna	Miss H. Kelesi and Miss J. Novotna 7–6, 2–6, 7–5		
4	Miss A. Grant and Miss S. T. Mair			Miss V. Milvidskaya and Miss L. Savchenko ① 6–3, 7–6
5	Miss N. Diaz and Miss M. Paz ③	Miss E. Reinach and Miss M. Reinach 6–1, 6–2		
6	Miss E. Reinach and Miss M. Reinach		Miss E. Reinach and Miss M. Reinach 6–2, 7–6	
7	Miss A. Betzner and Miss I. Cueto	Miss A. Betzner and Miss I. Cueto 6–3, 7–6		
8	Miss B. A. Borneo and Miss J. Louis			
9	Miss L. Garrone and Miss K. Maleeva	Miss E. Krapl and Miss M. Yokota w o		
10	Miss E. Krapl and Miss M. Yokota		Miss C. Kuhlman and Miss S. Rehe w o	
11	Miss C. Kuhlman and Miss S. Rehe	Miss C. Kuhlman and Miss S. Rehe 7–5, 6–4		
12	Miss R. Mentz and Miss K. Schuurmans ④			Miss C. Kuhlman and Miss S. Rehe 6–0, 6–3
13	Miss C. Anderholm and Miss M. Lundquist	Miss E. Iida and Miss A. Kijimuta 2–6, 6–3, 6–3		
14	Miss E. Iida and Miss A. Kijimuta		Miss E. Iida and Miss A. Kijimuta 6–4, 4–6, 6–1	
15	Miss P. Moreno and Miss J. Saberon	Miss D. Ketelaar and Miss S. Schilder ② 6–0, 7–6		
16	Miss D. Ketelaar and Miss S. Schilder ②			

Winner: Miss C. Kuhlman and Miss S. Rehe 6–3, 5–7, 6–4

PHOTOGRAPHIC ACKNOWLEDGEMENTS

The majority of photographs in this book were taken by Tommy Hindley. Other photographic credits are as follows: Allsport: 9, 10, 11 (second right), 19 (below), 27, 62, 66 (top left), 87 (left), 89 (below), 104 (below left), 105, 118/119, 125, 129, 133, 135; Associated Newspapers: (Ted Blackbrow) 6 (left and centre below), 64 (left), 84, 87 (right), 108, 109, 112, (Bill Cross) 6 (centre top), 24, (Keith Dobney) 56, (Monty Fresco) 83; Associated Sports Photography: (George Herringshaw) 11 (third right), 18 (below), 19 (top), 72, 101 (top), 152; Arthur Cole: 66/67 (below), 101 (below), 116 (top left), 138 (below), 144; Michael Cole: 6 (top left), 60 (right), 65, 123 (left), 132, 136, 138 (top); Steve Hale: 33 (below), 116 (top right); Peter Jay: 124; Jack Kay: 110 (the winning photograph from the 'Special event – Wimbledon' Kodak Black and White Photography Awards 1984; Carol Newsom: 6 (top right); Roy Peters: 18 (top), 75, 107, 154, 157: Peter Skirgley: 2/3.